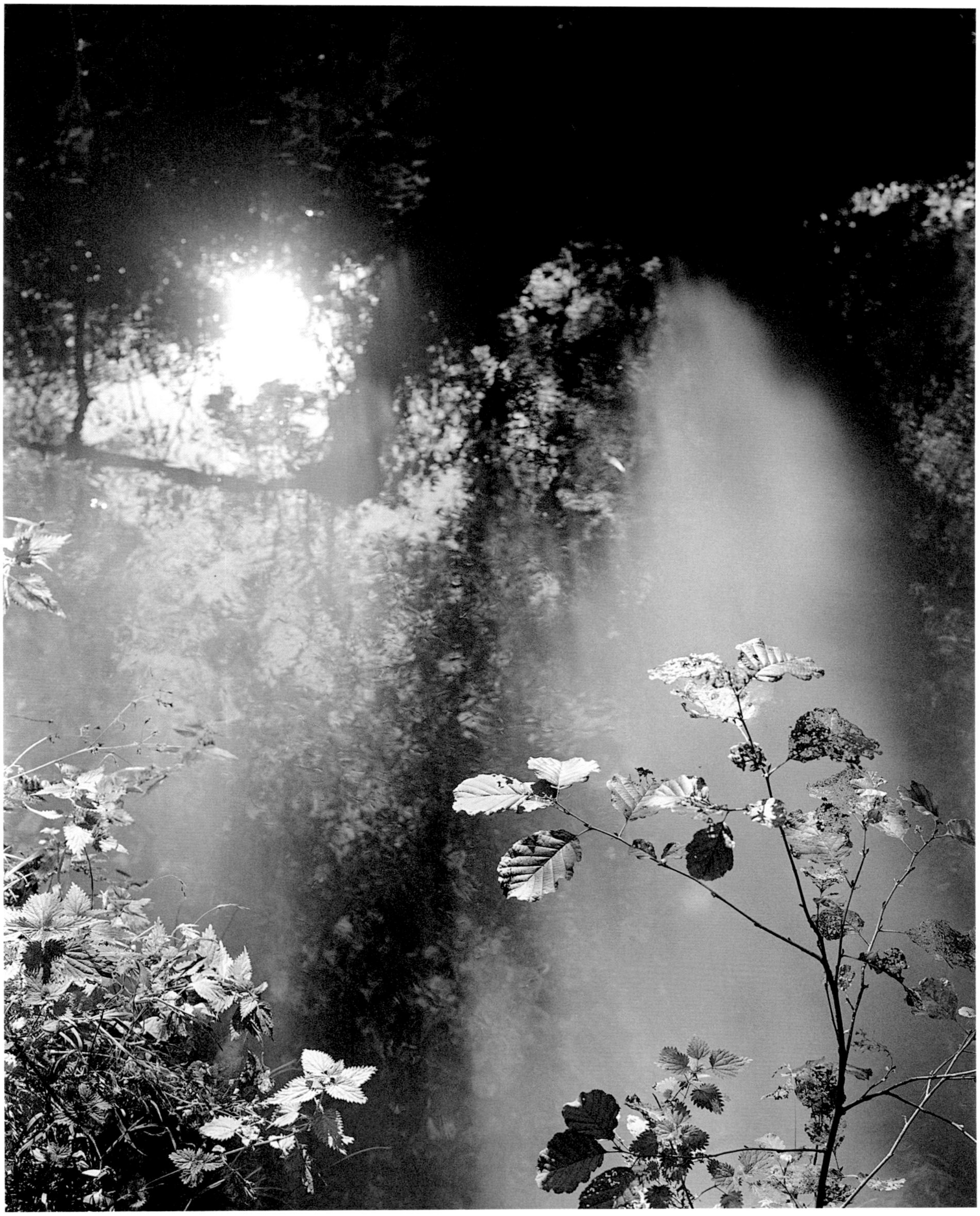

Faultlines

John Volynchook

GOST

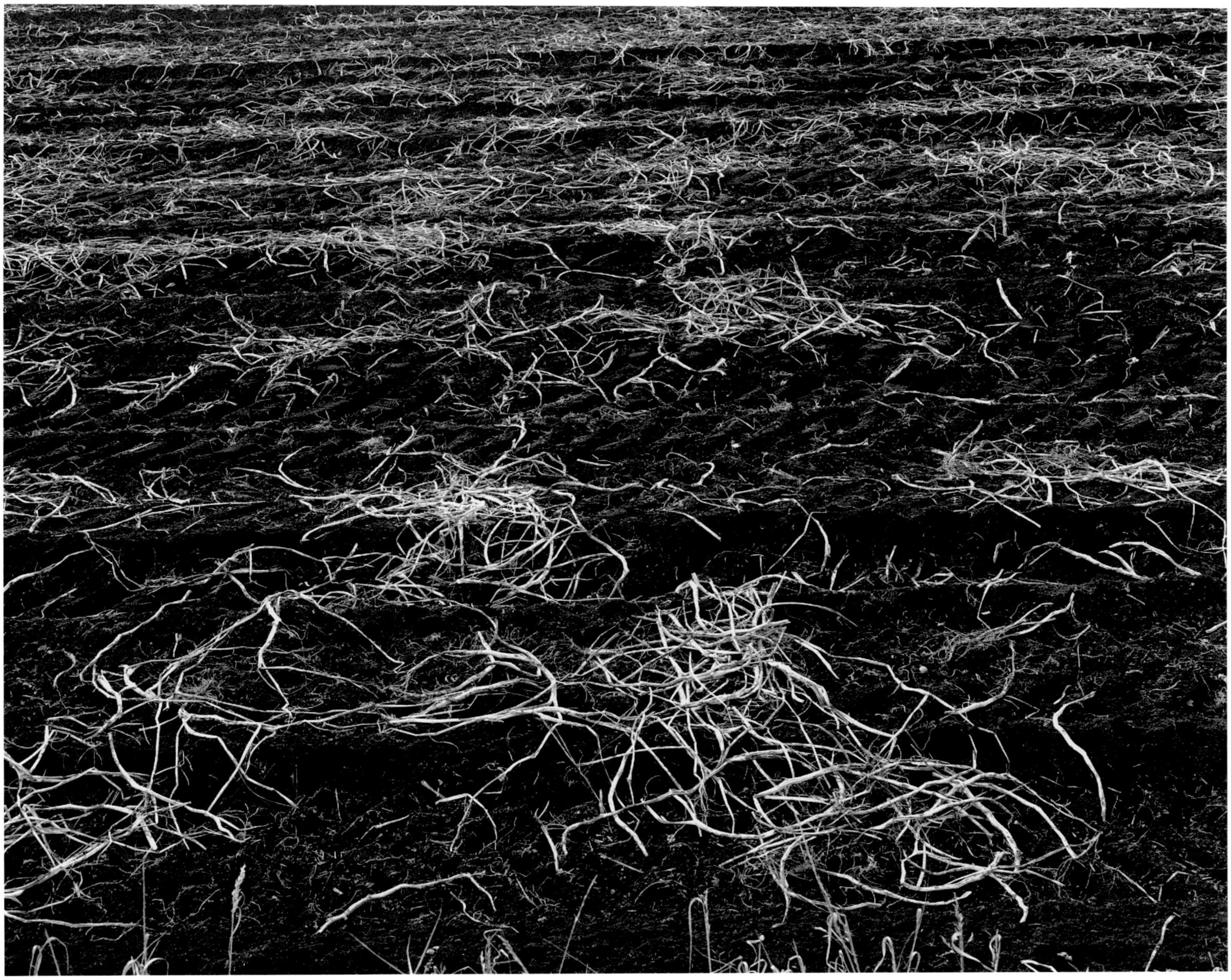

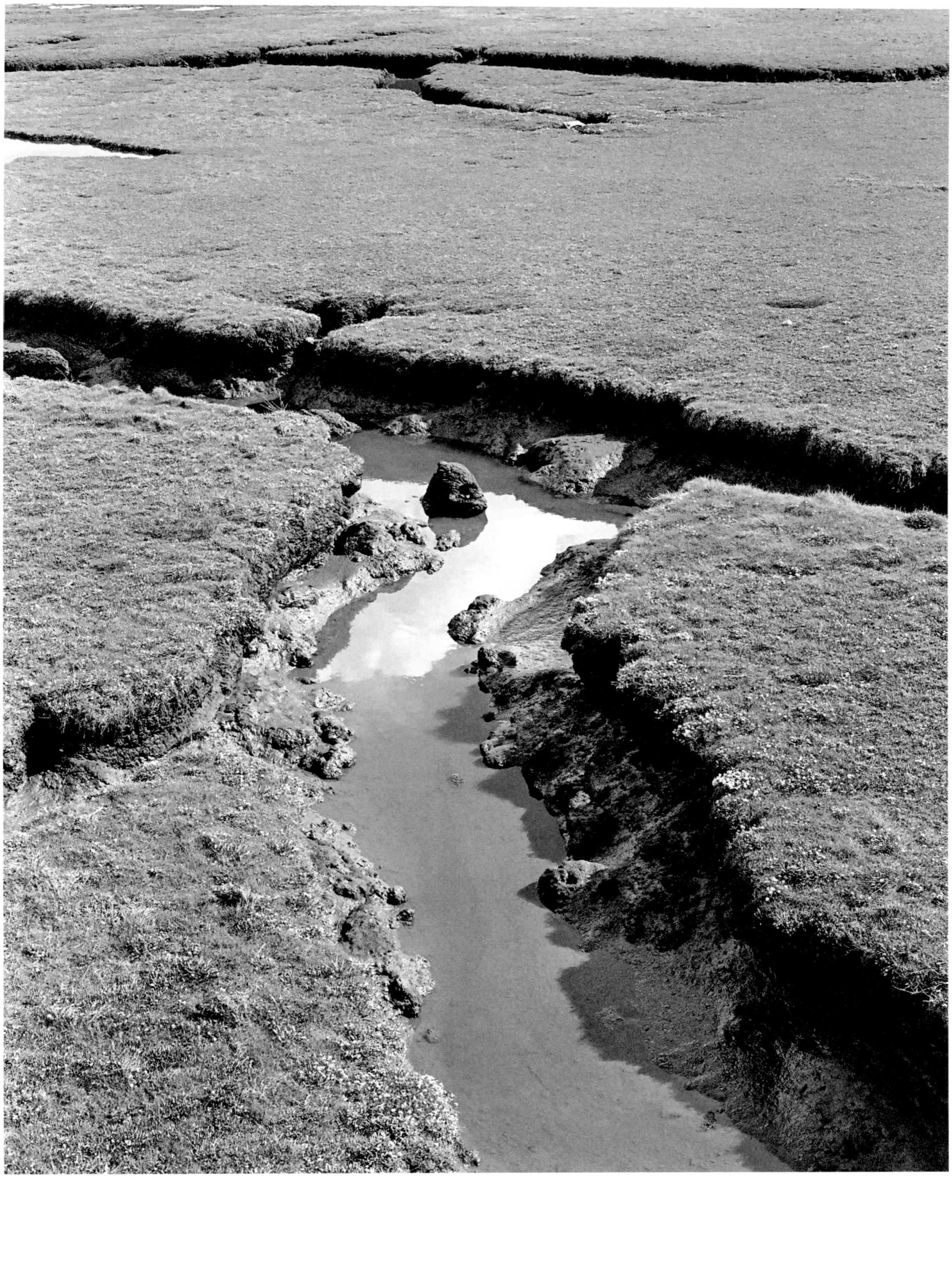

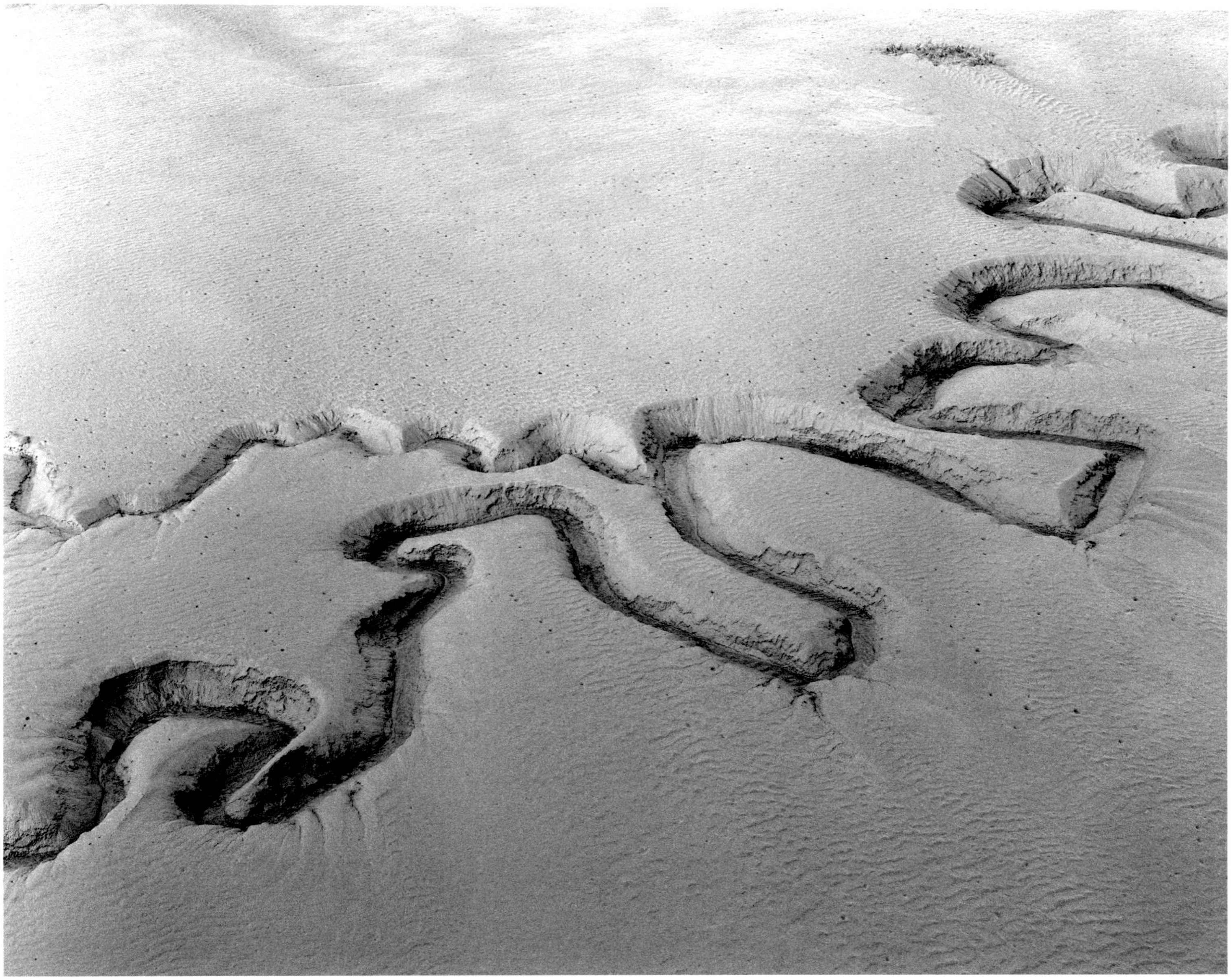

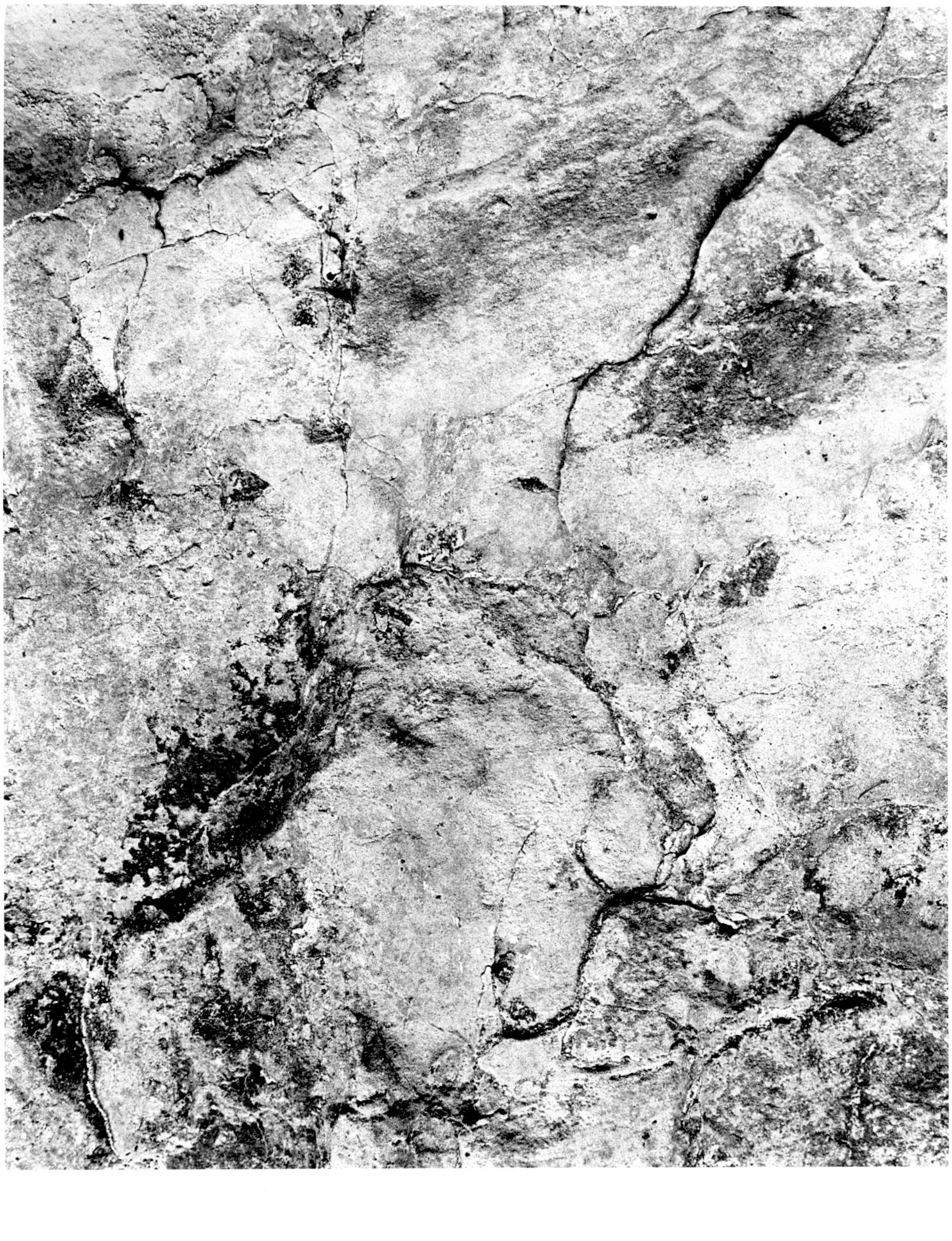

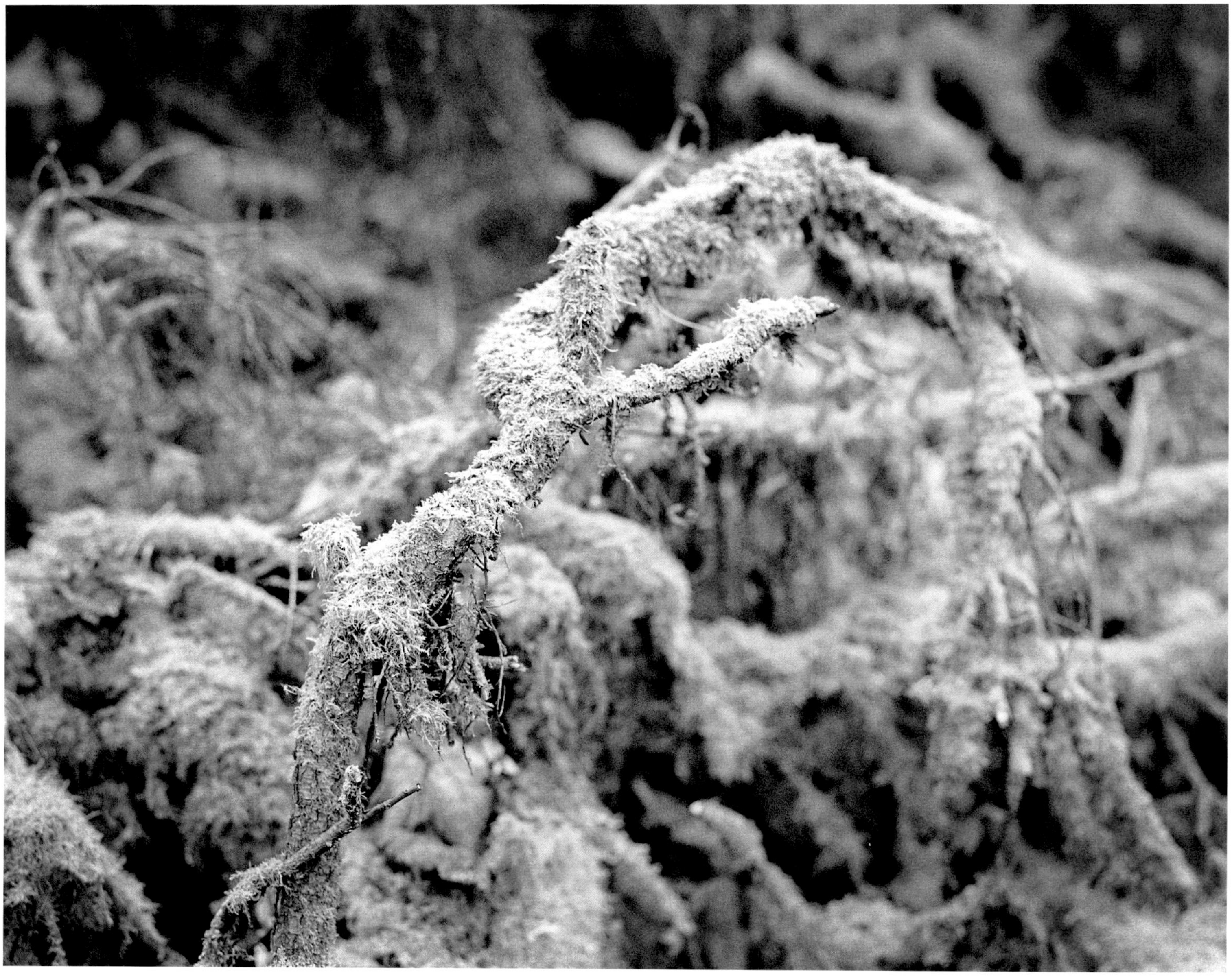

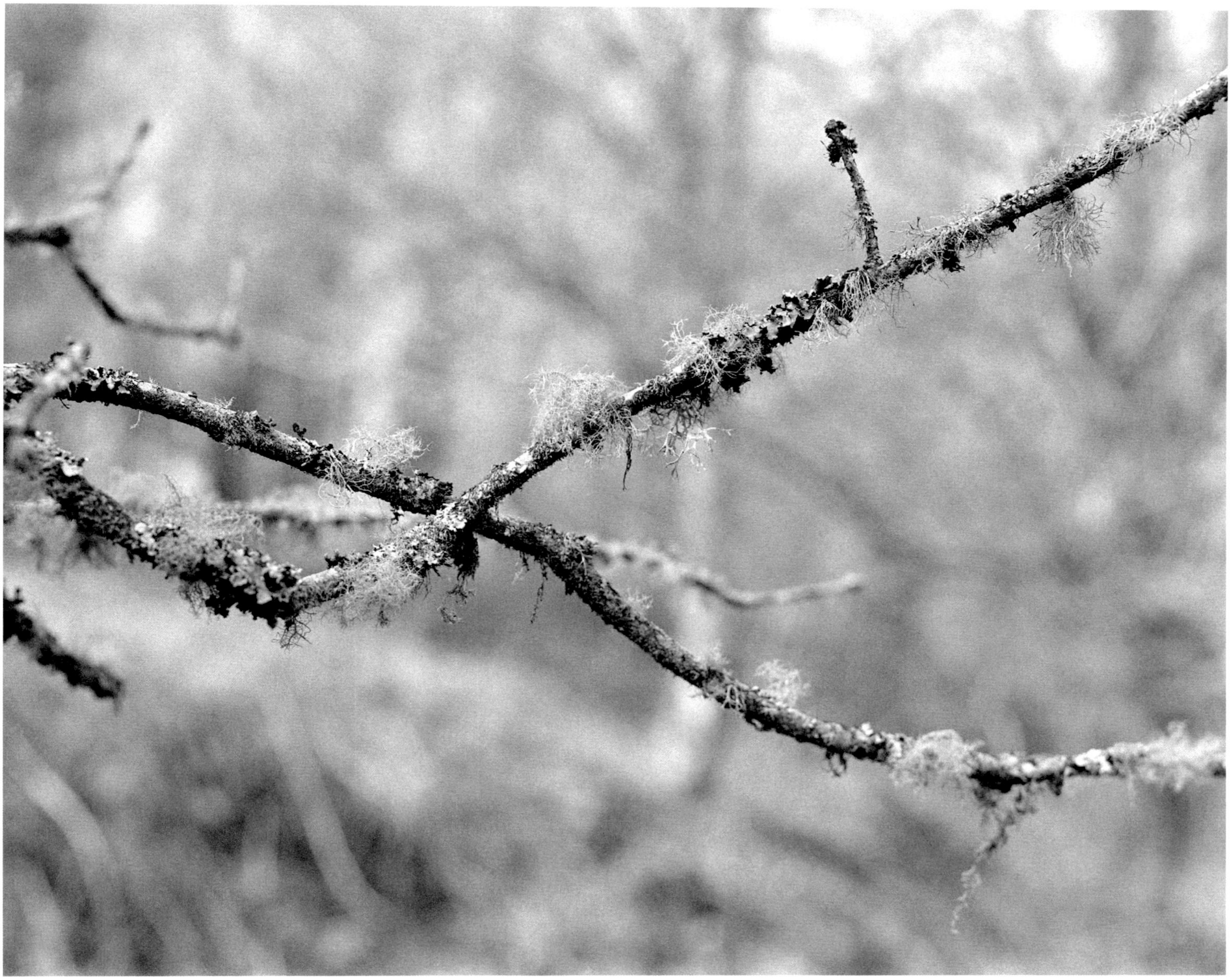

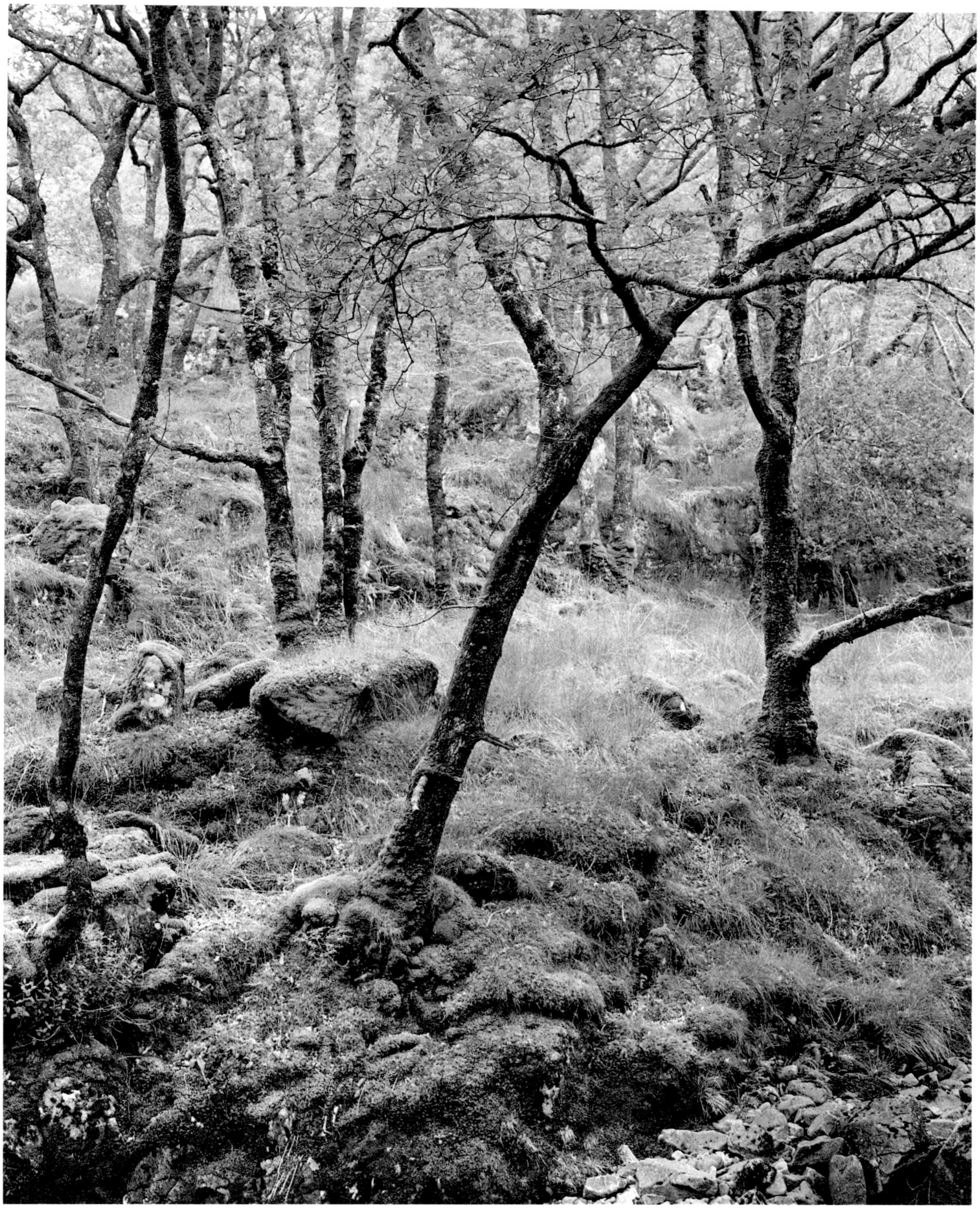

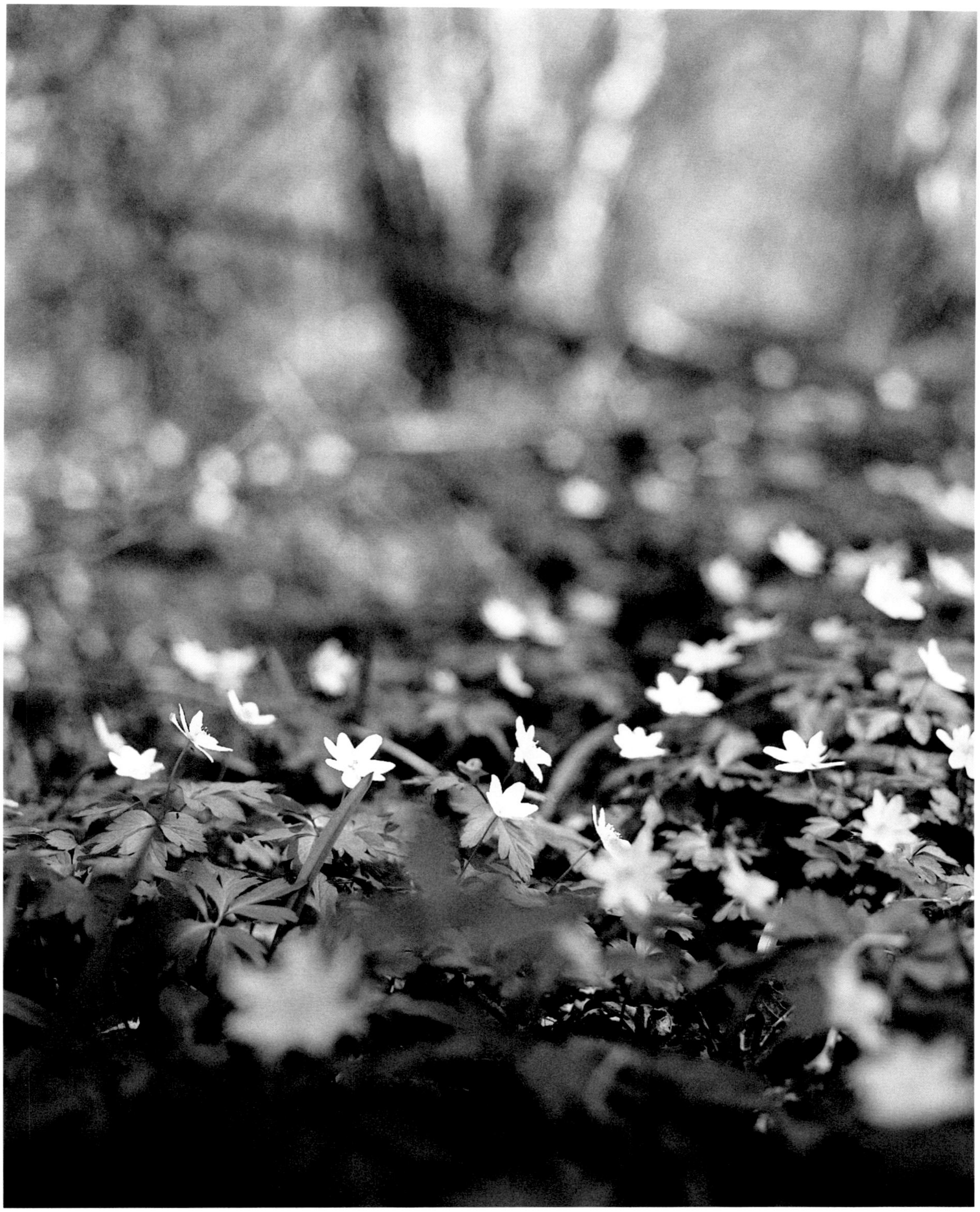

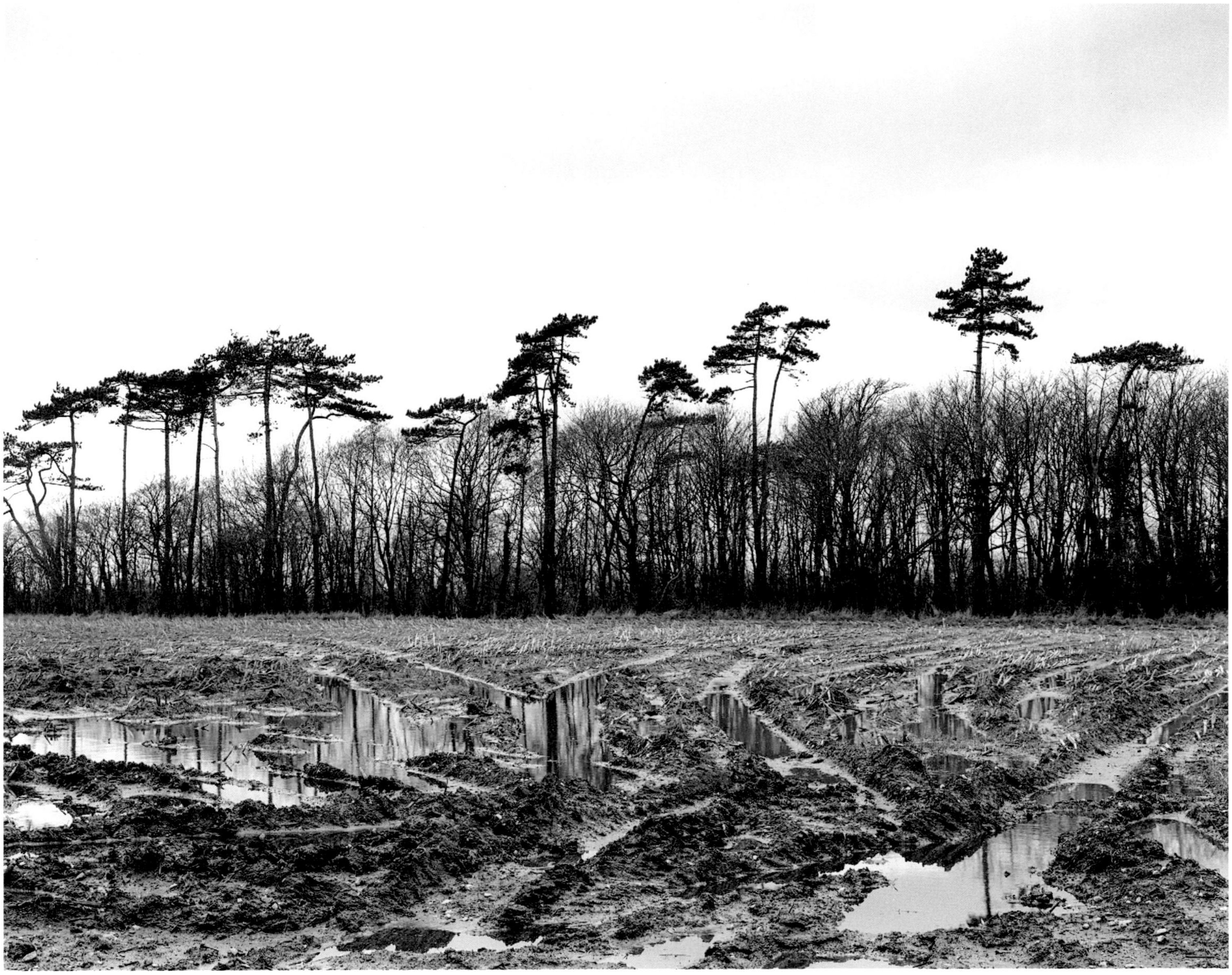

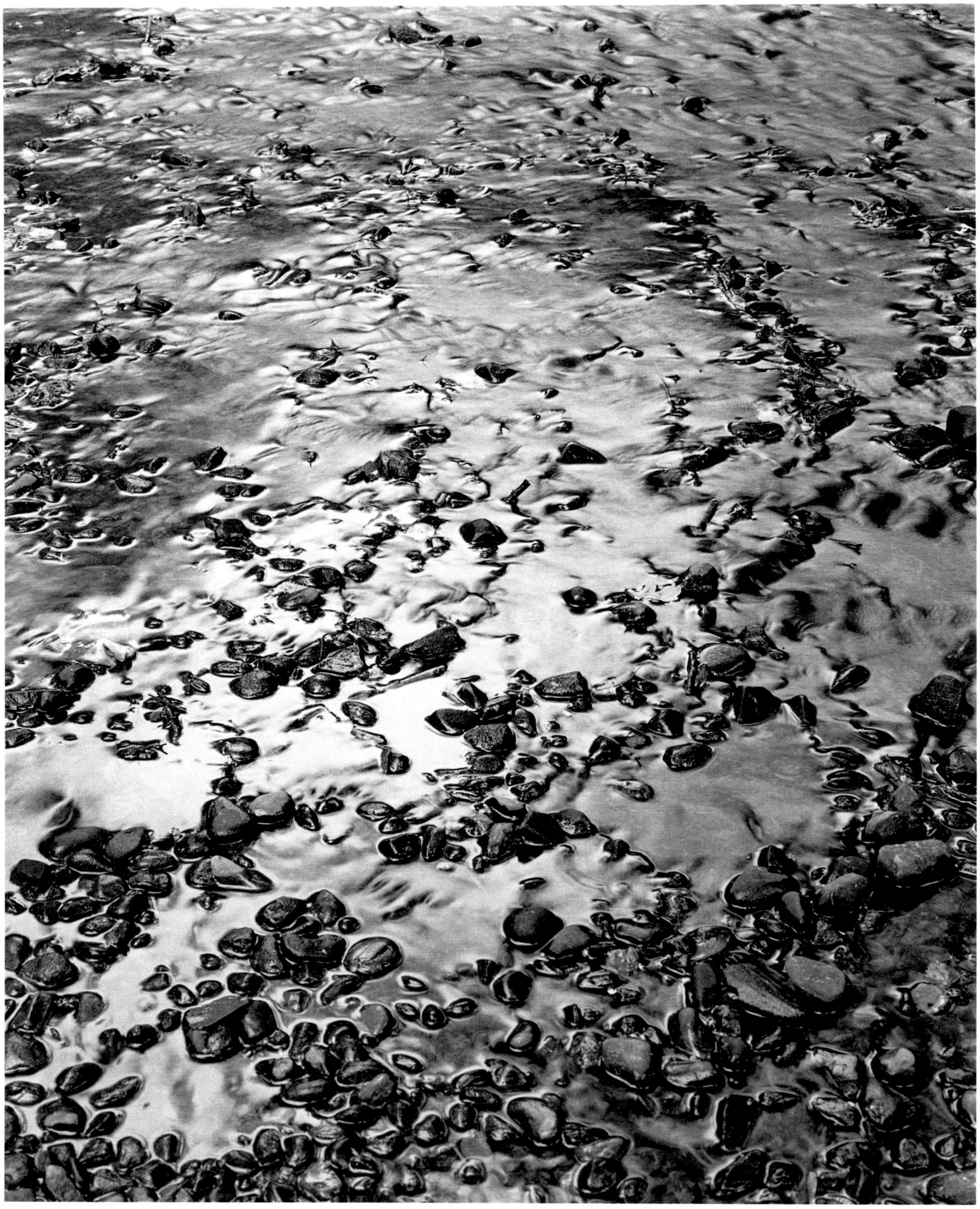

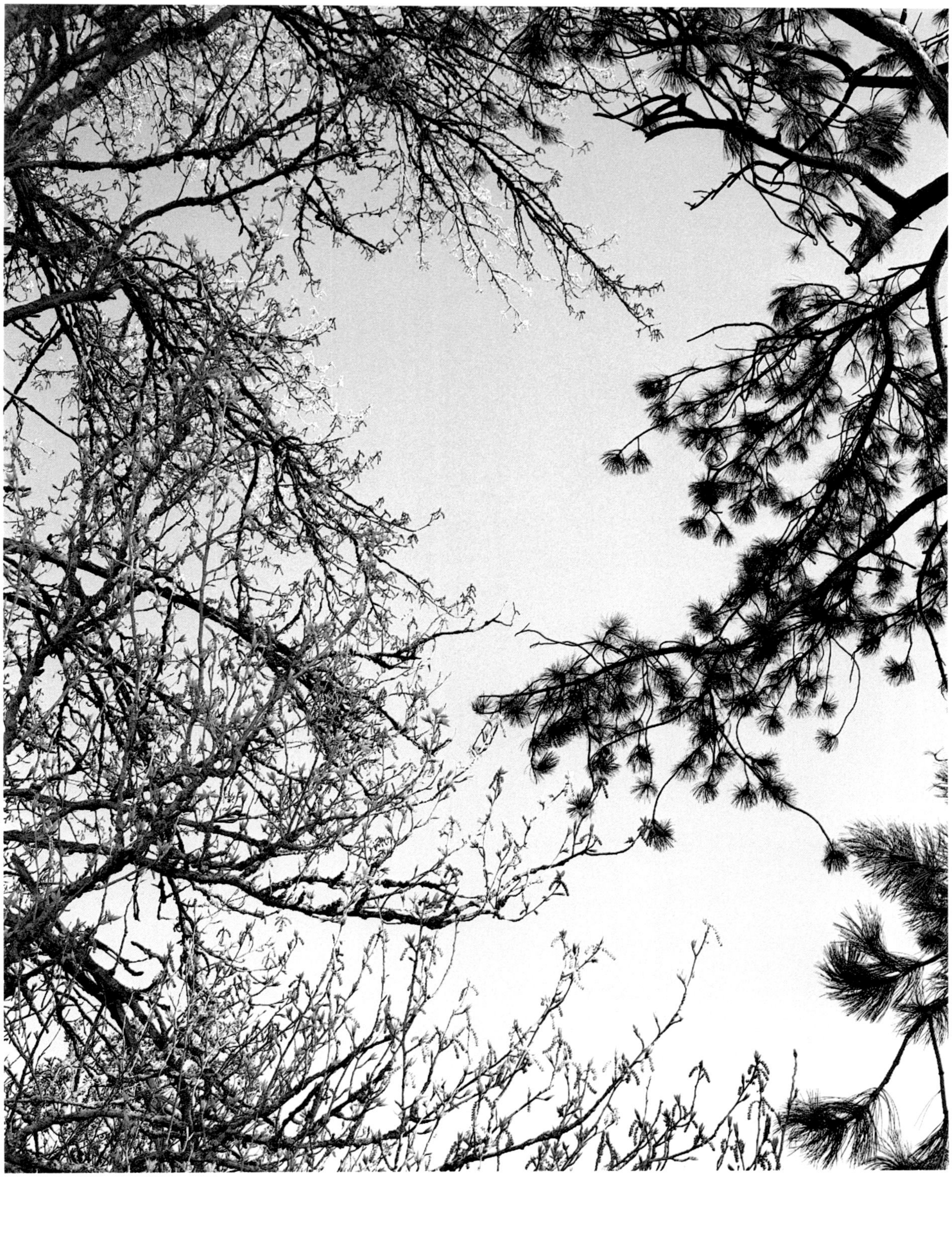

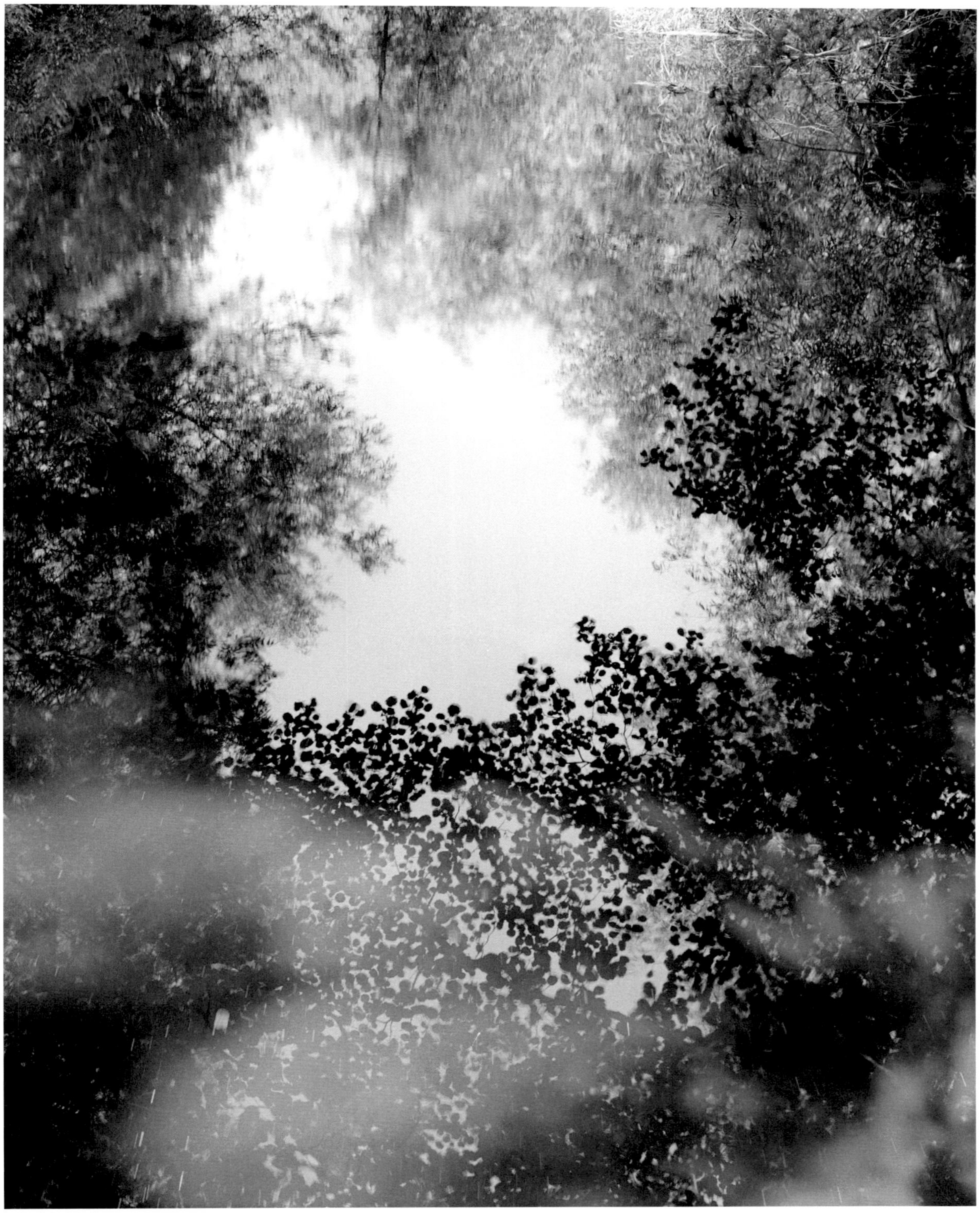

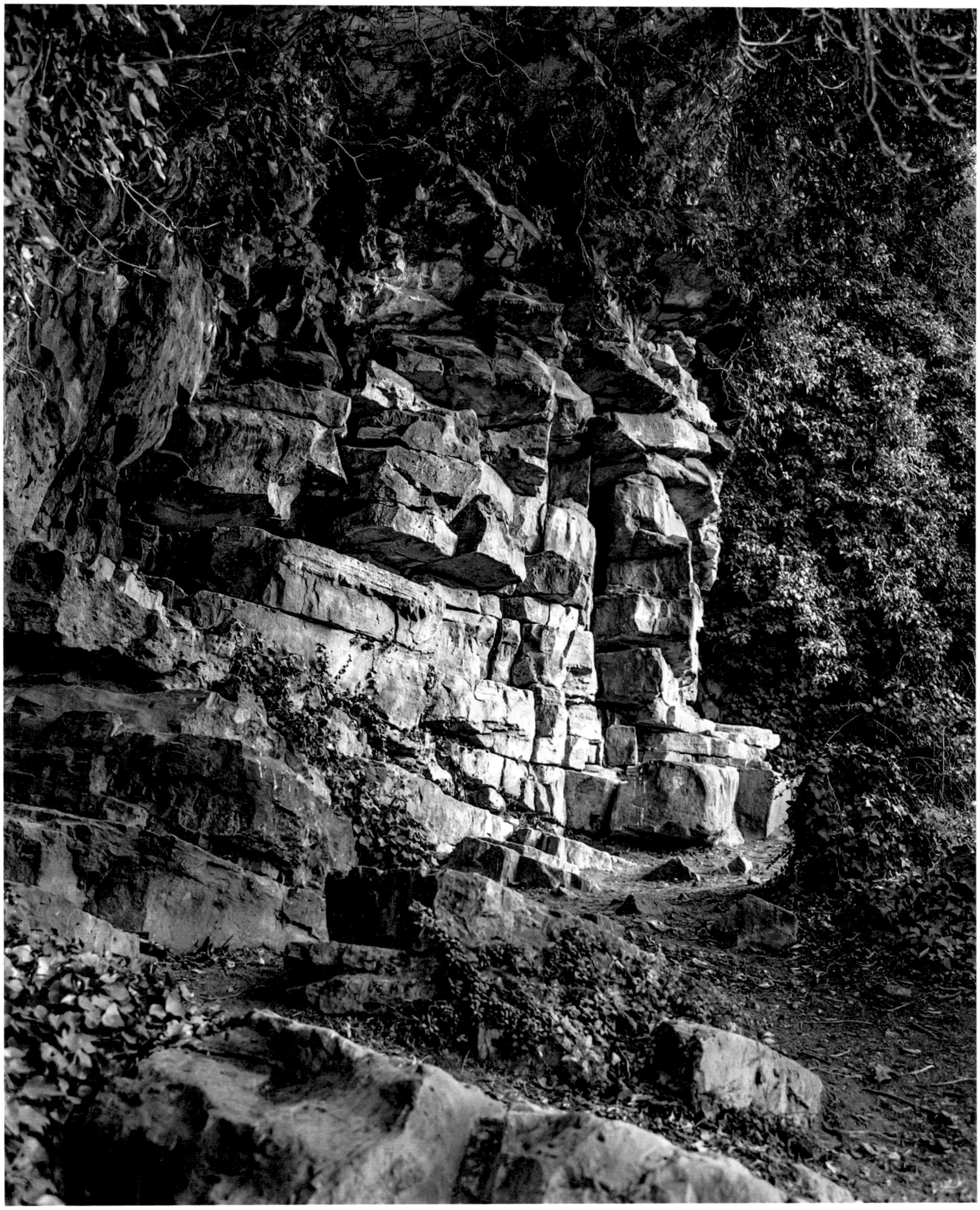

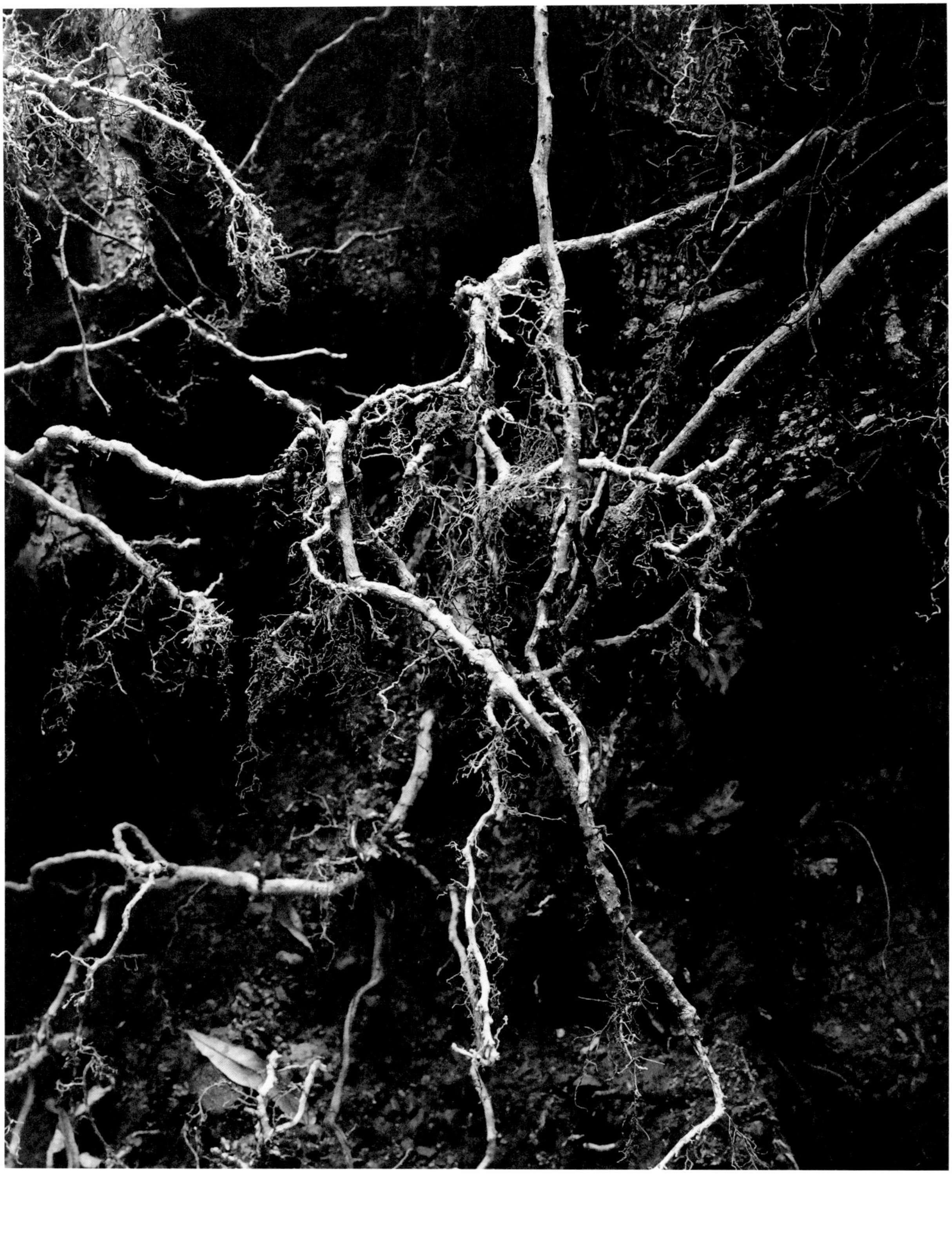

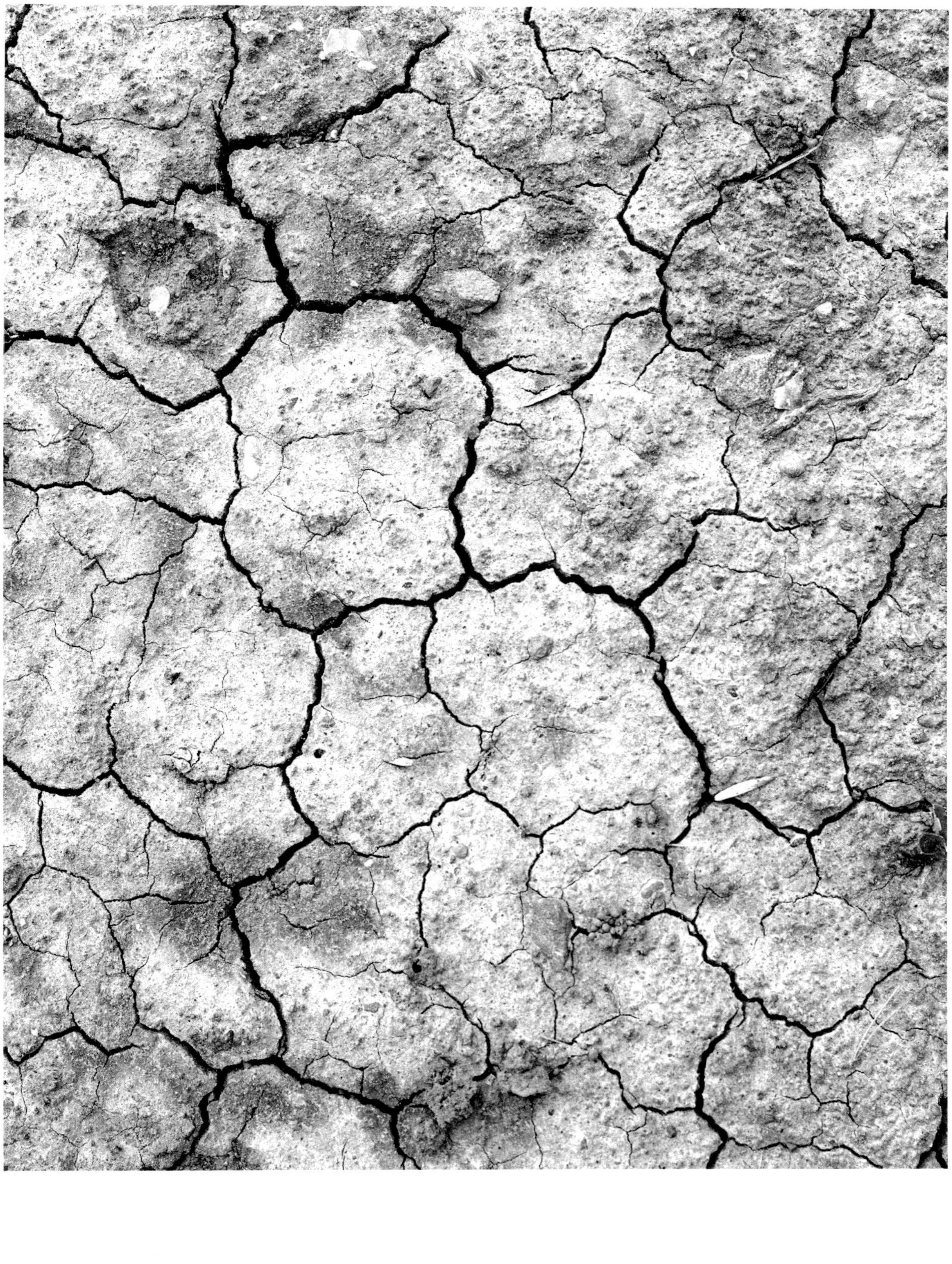

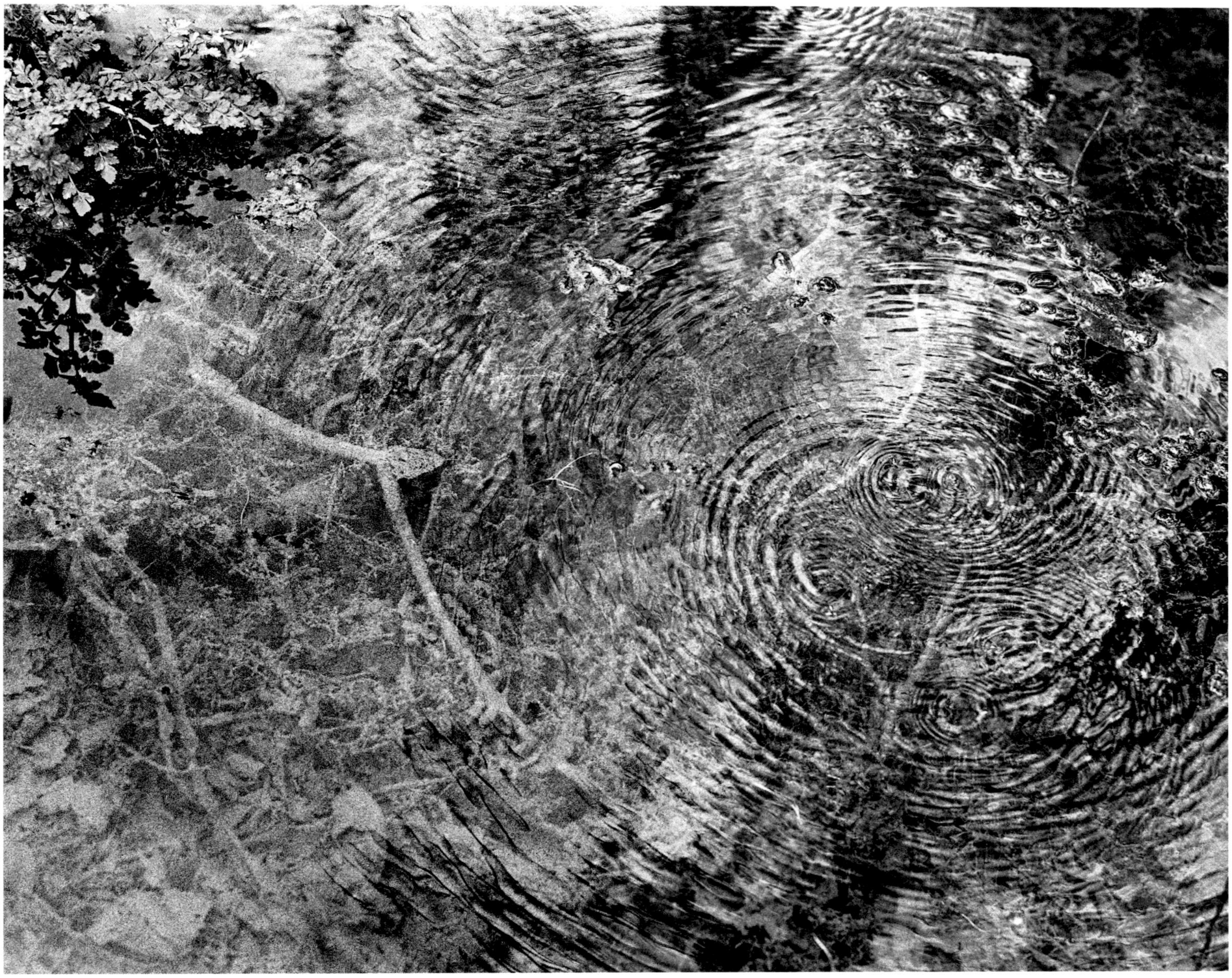

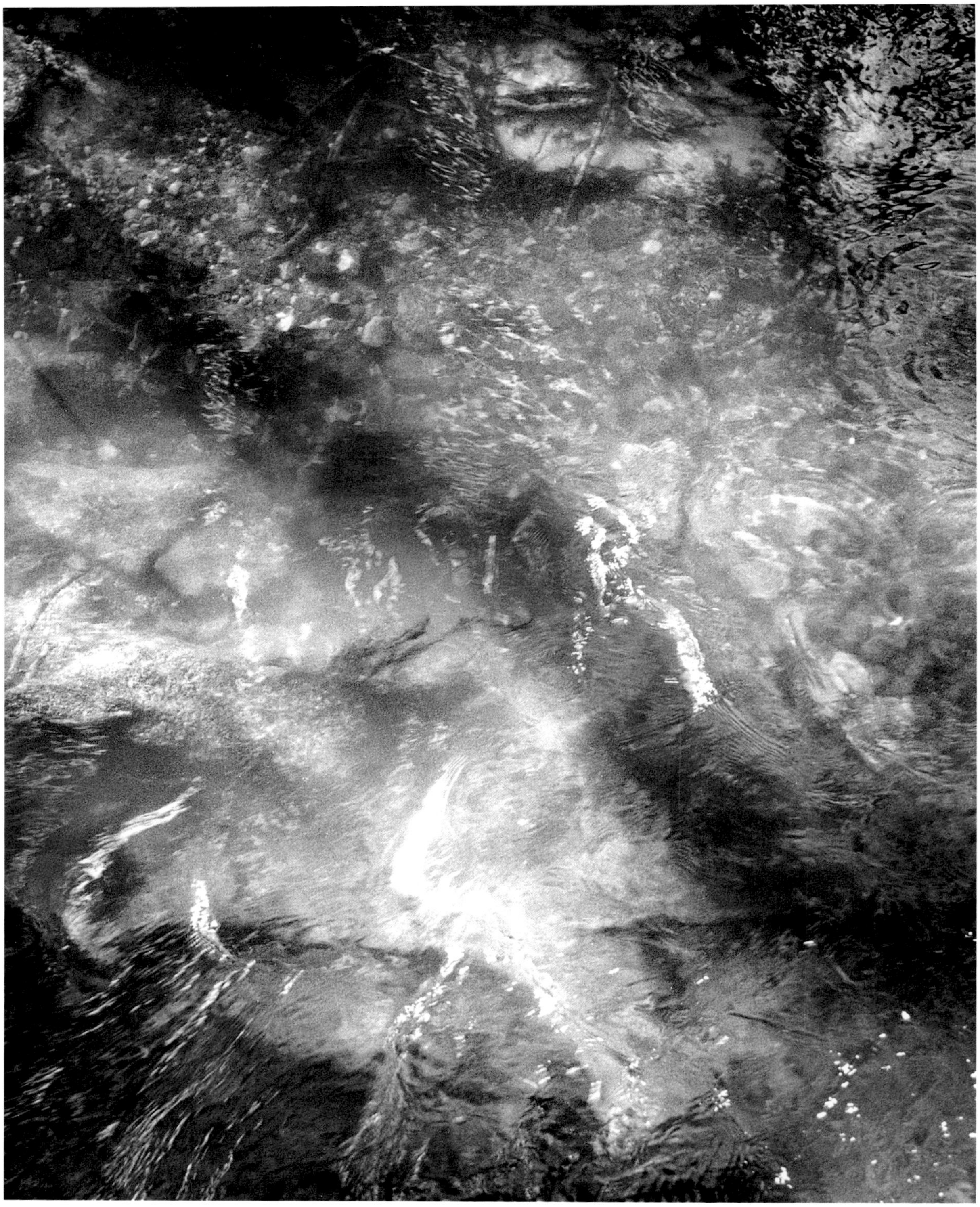

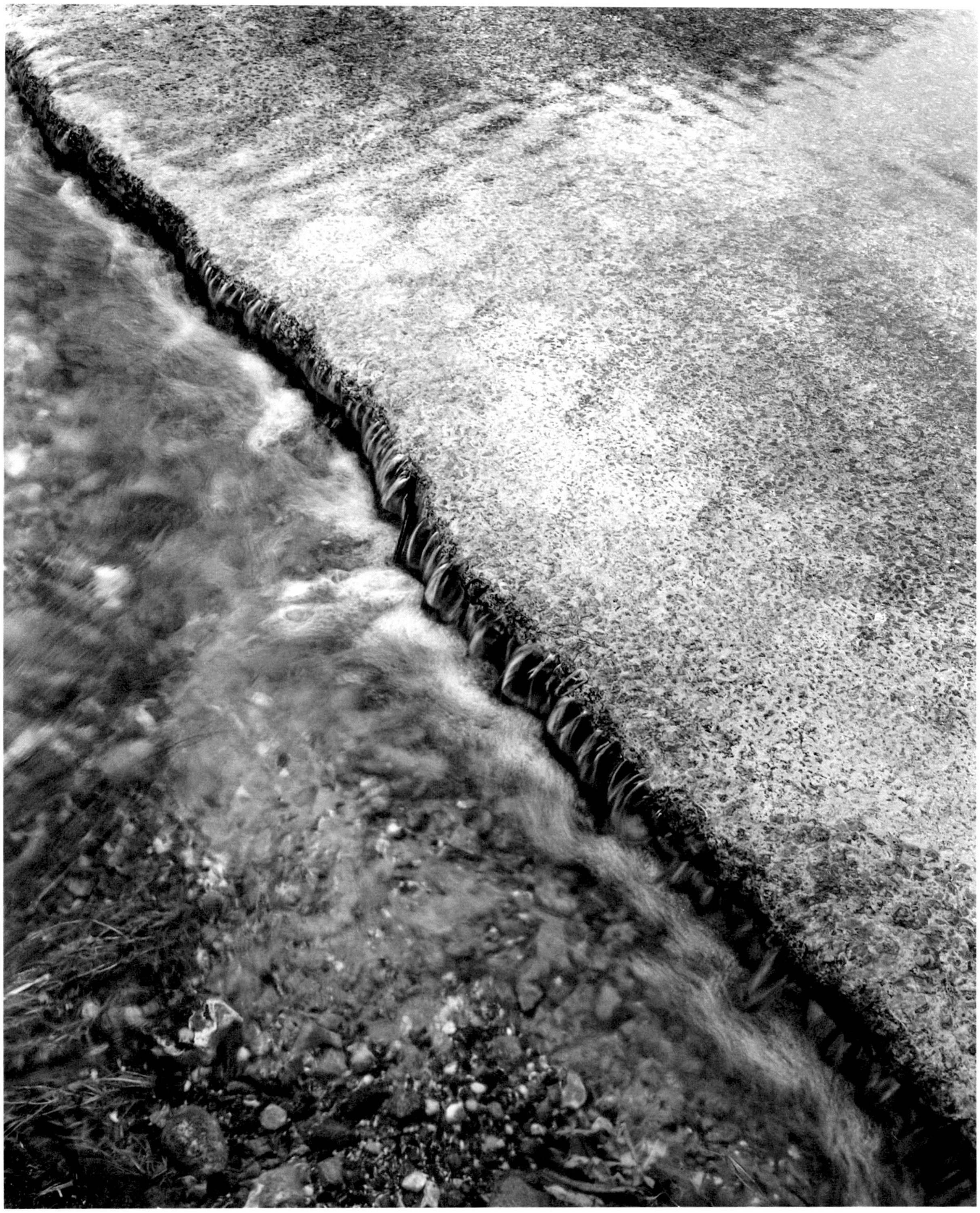

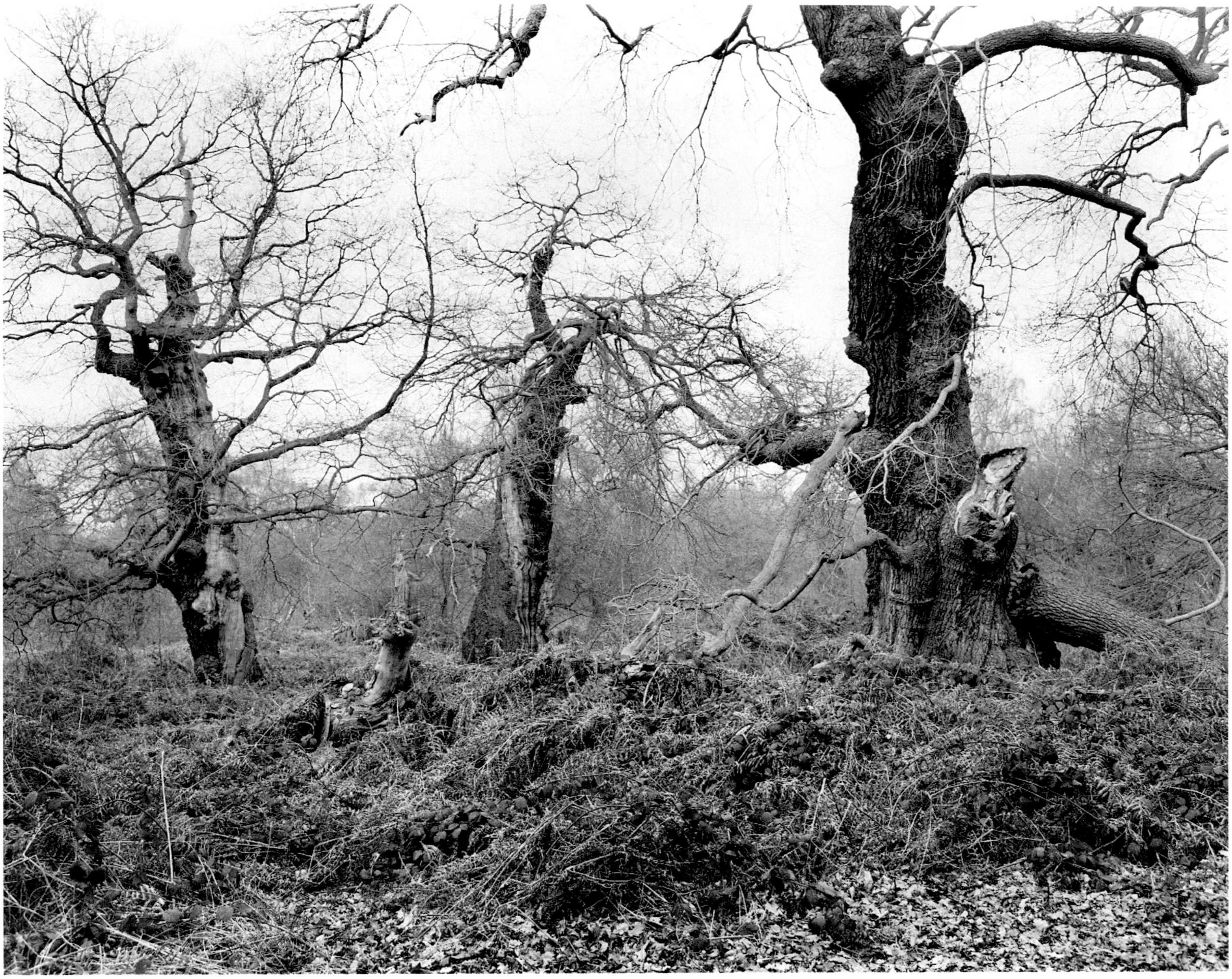

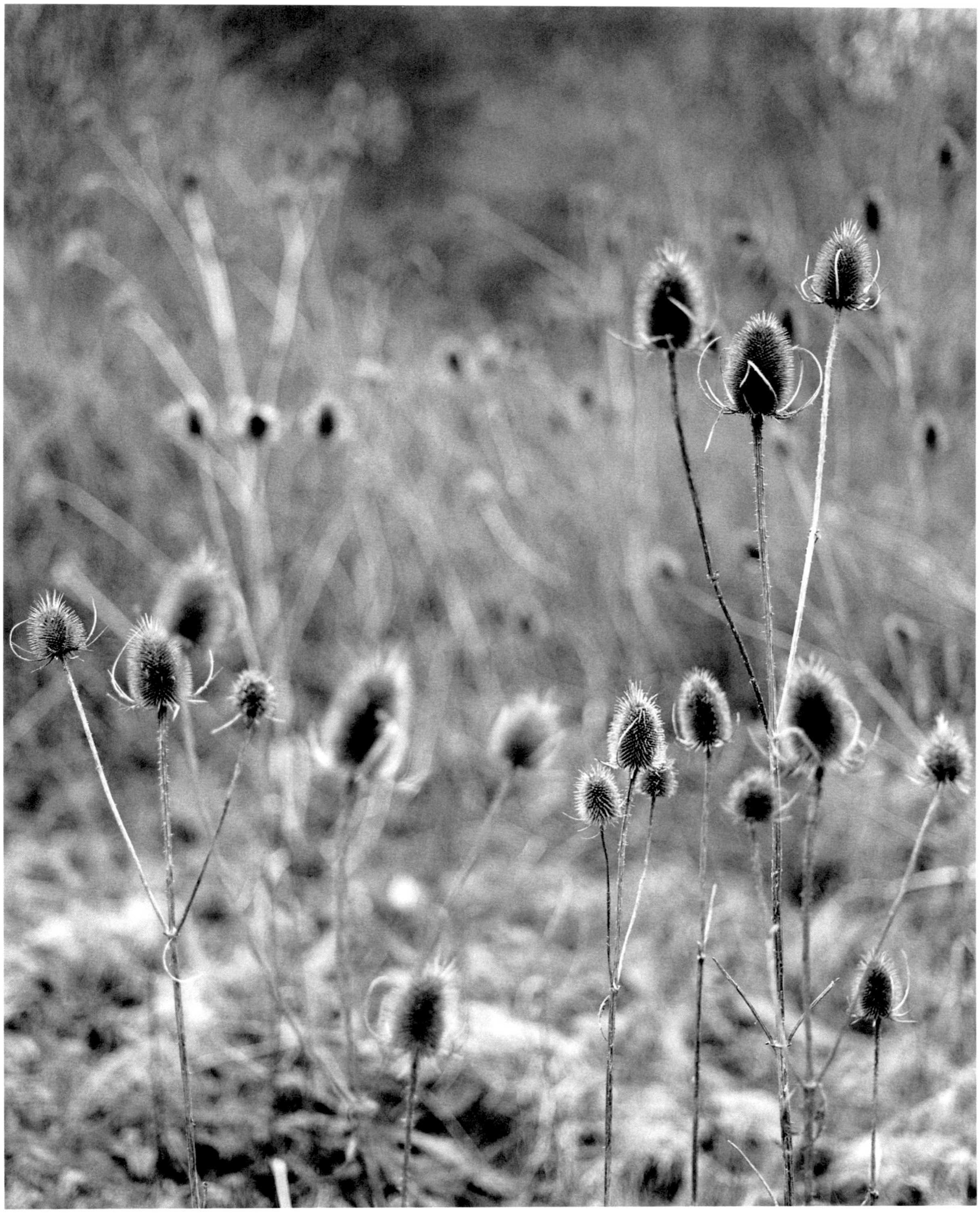

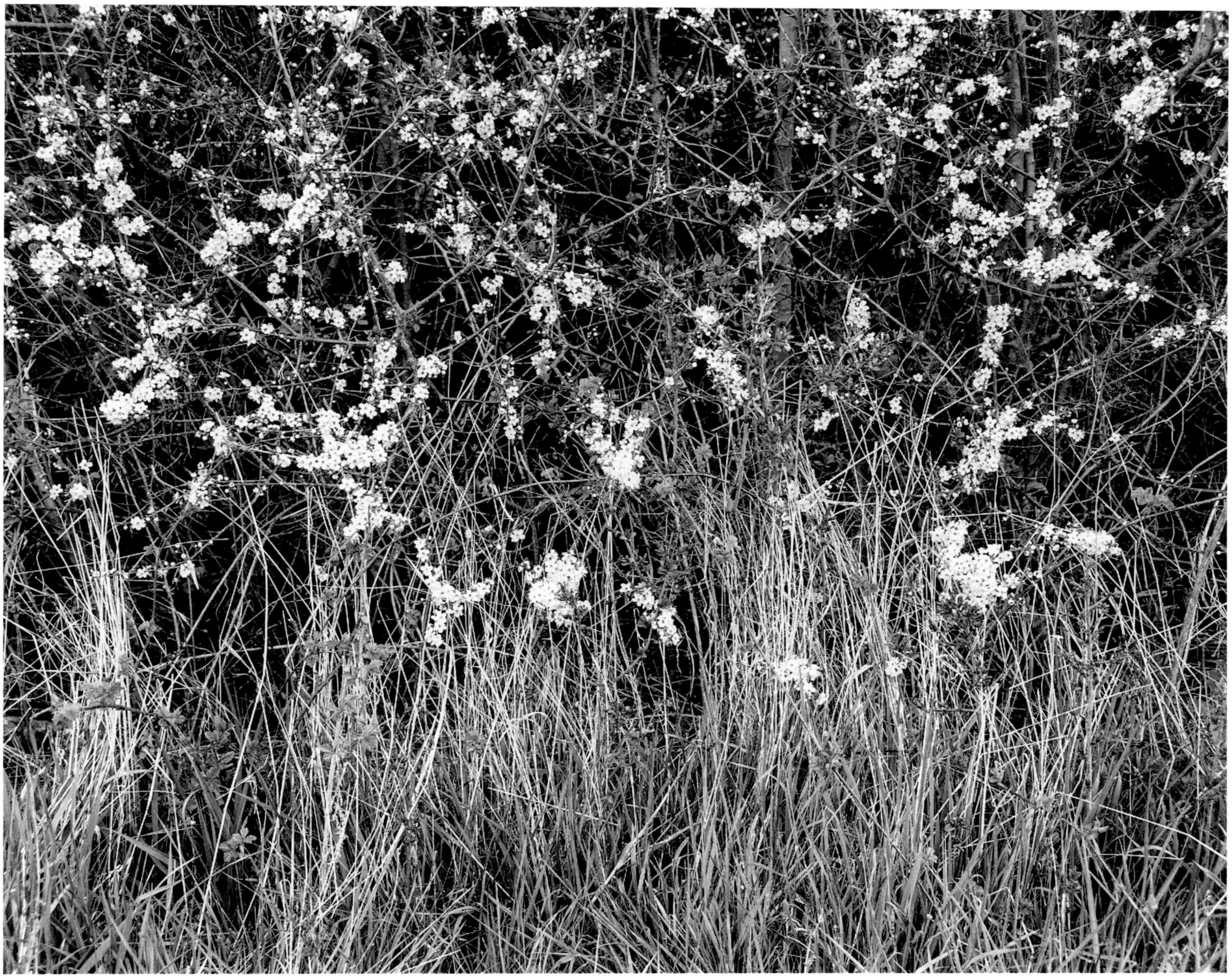

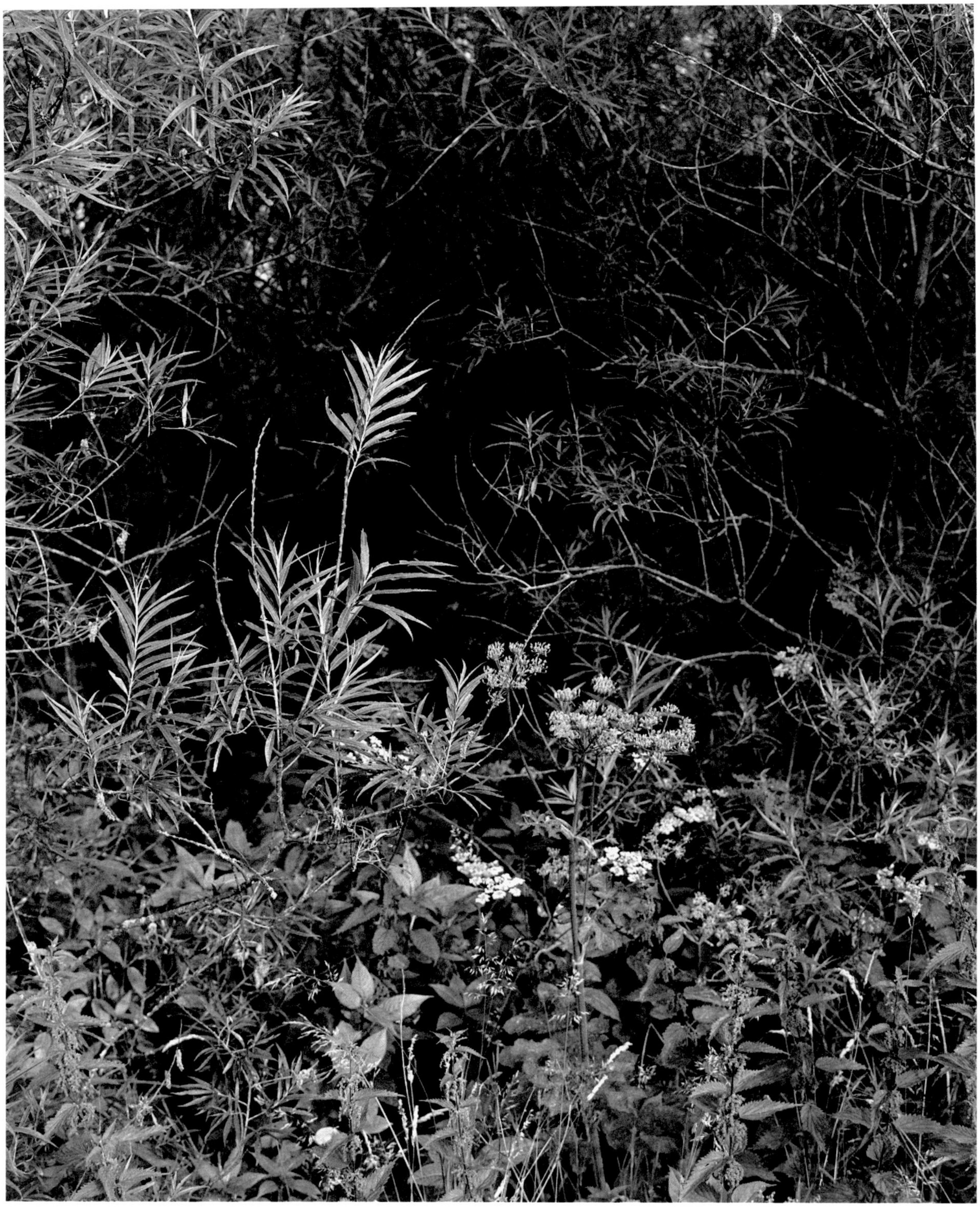

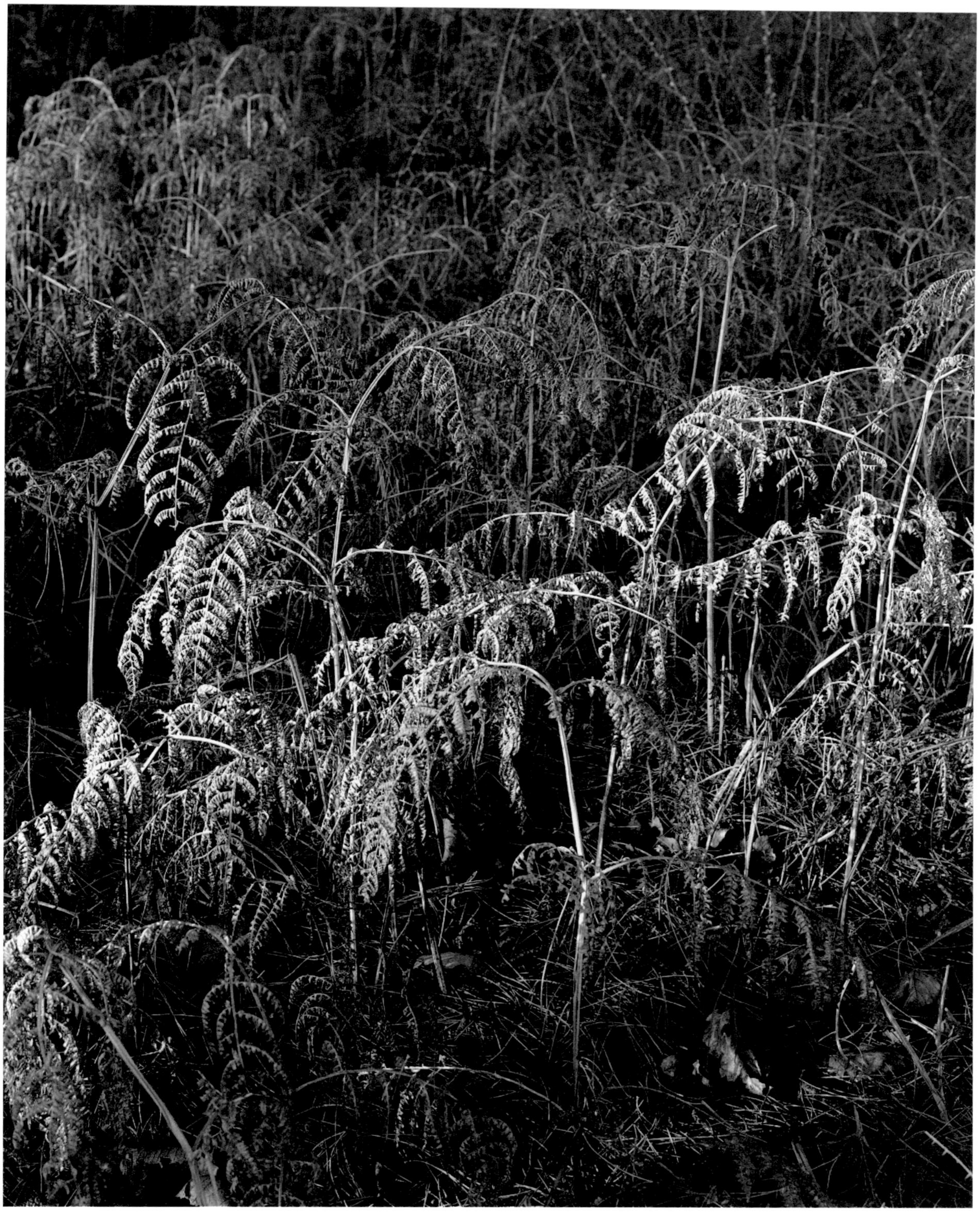

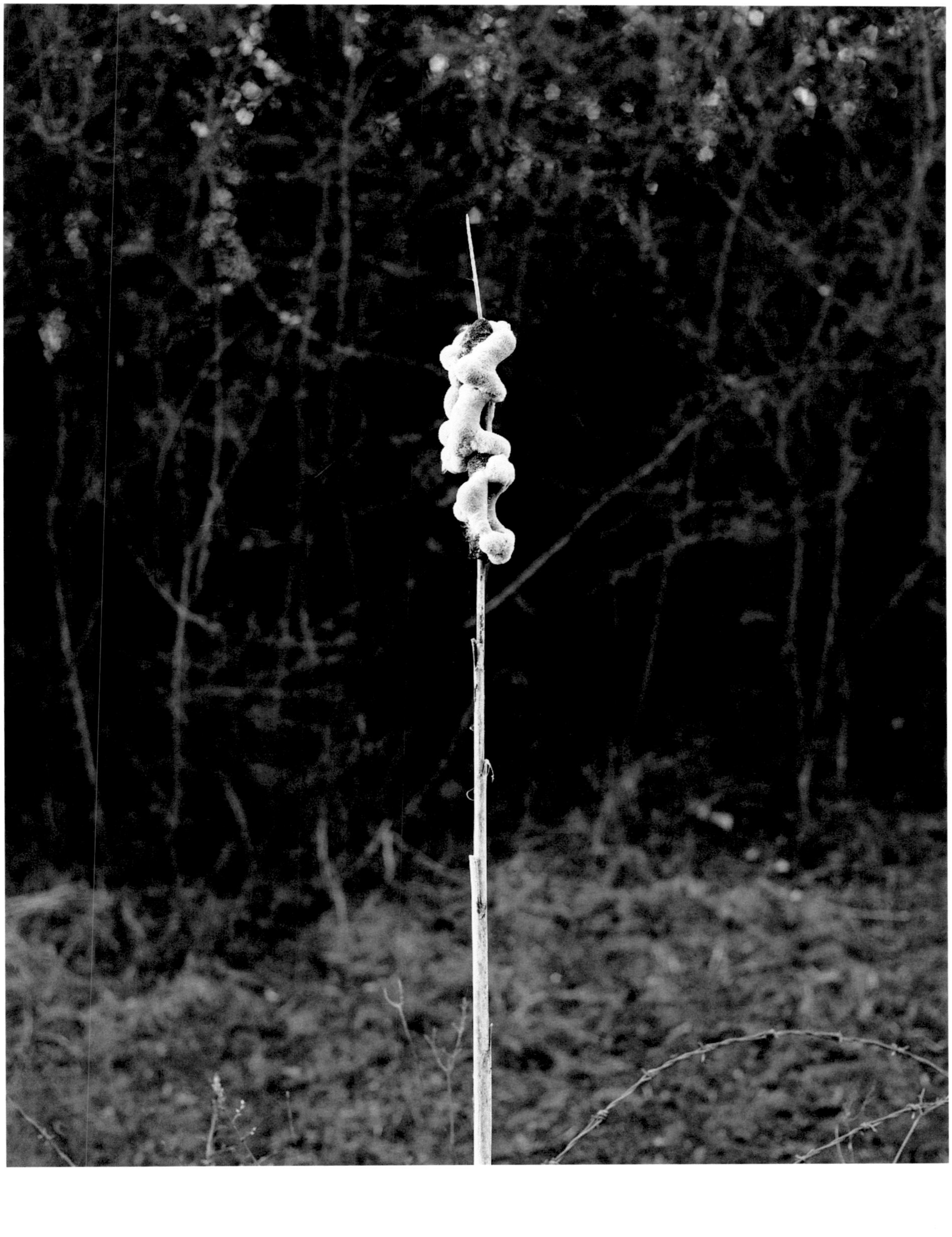

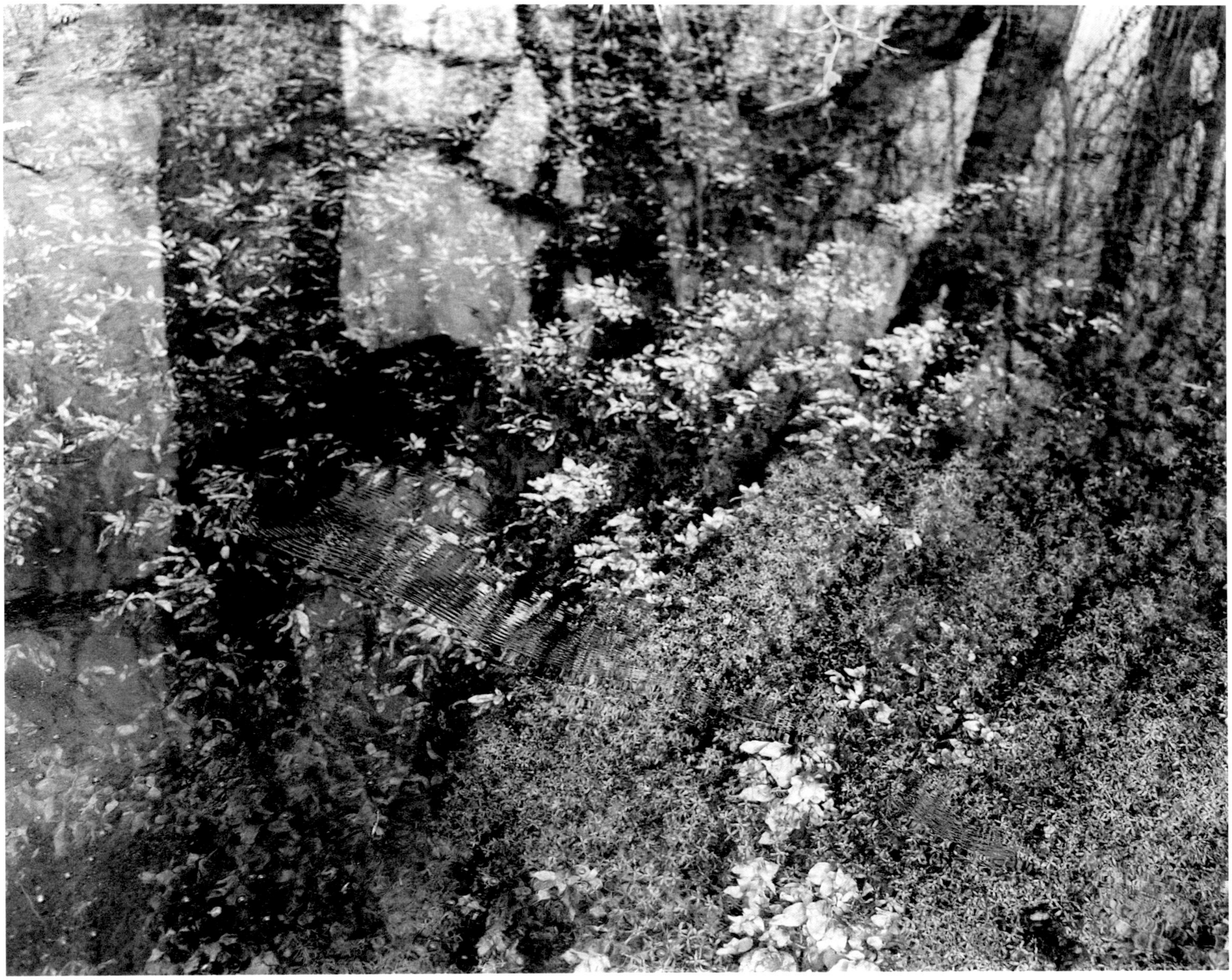

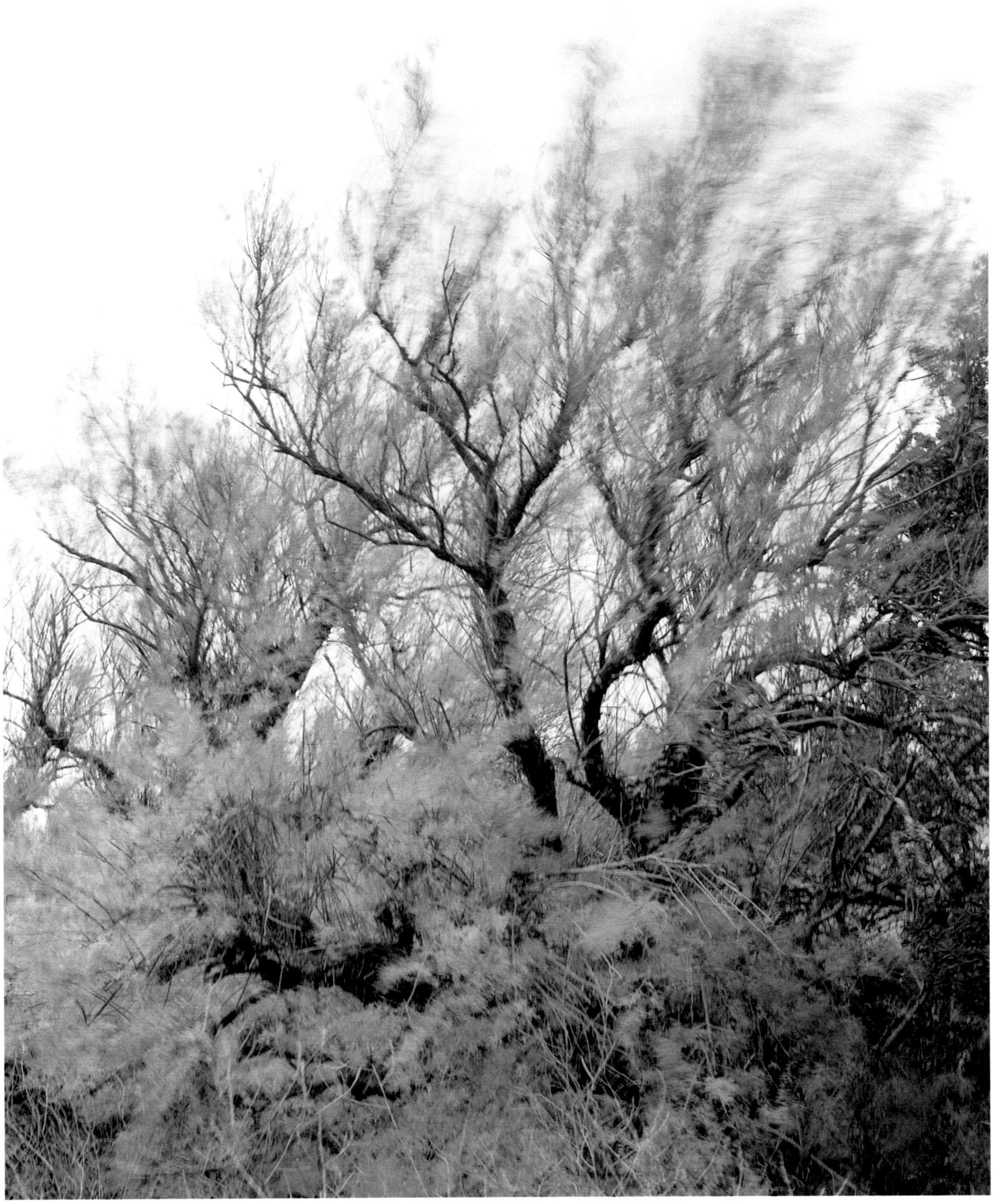

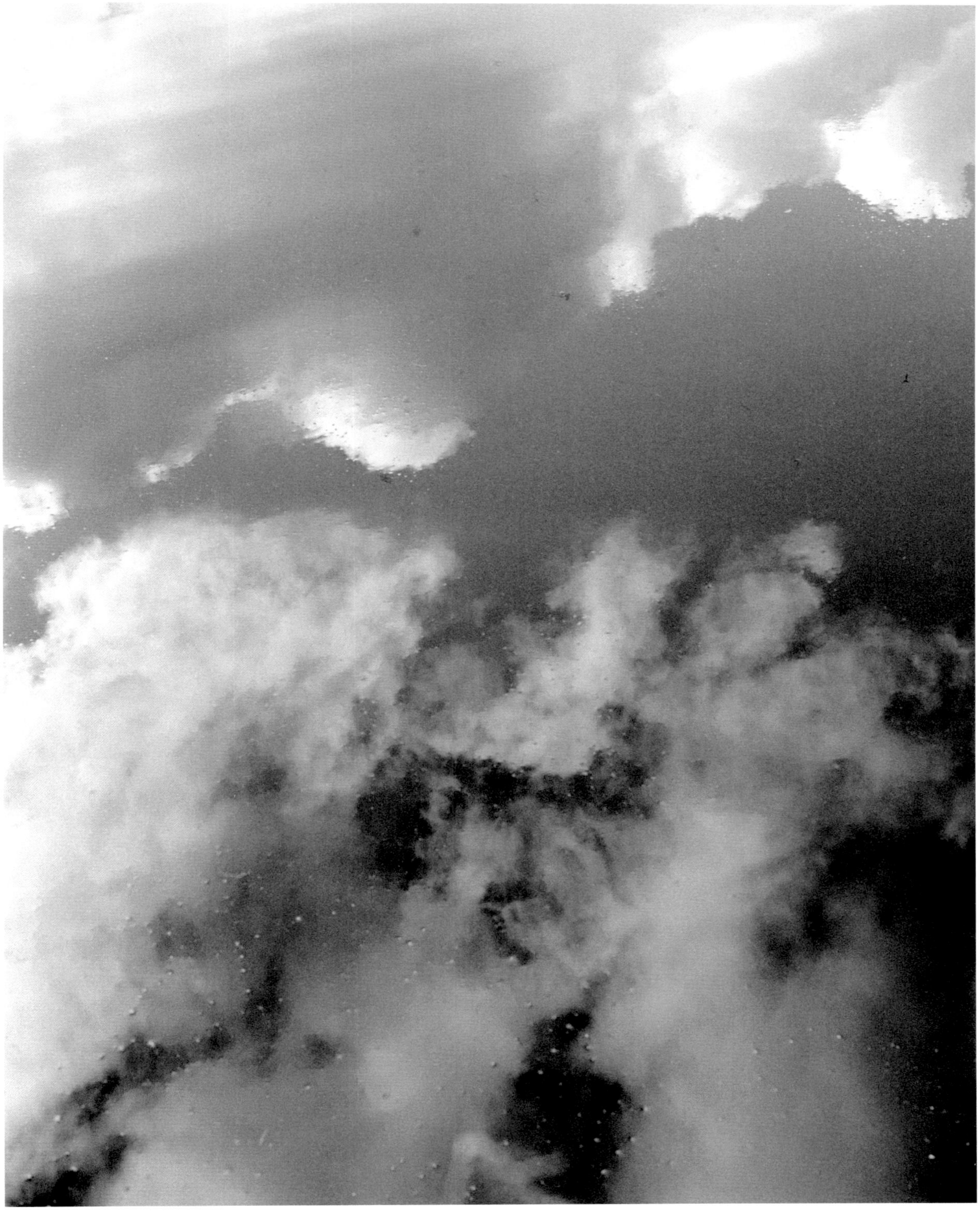

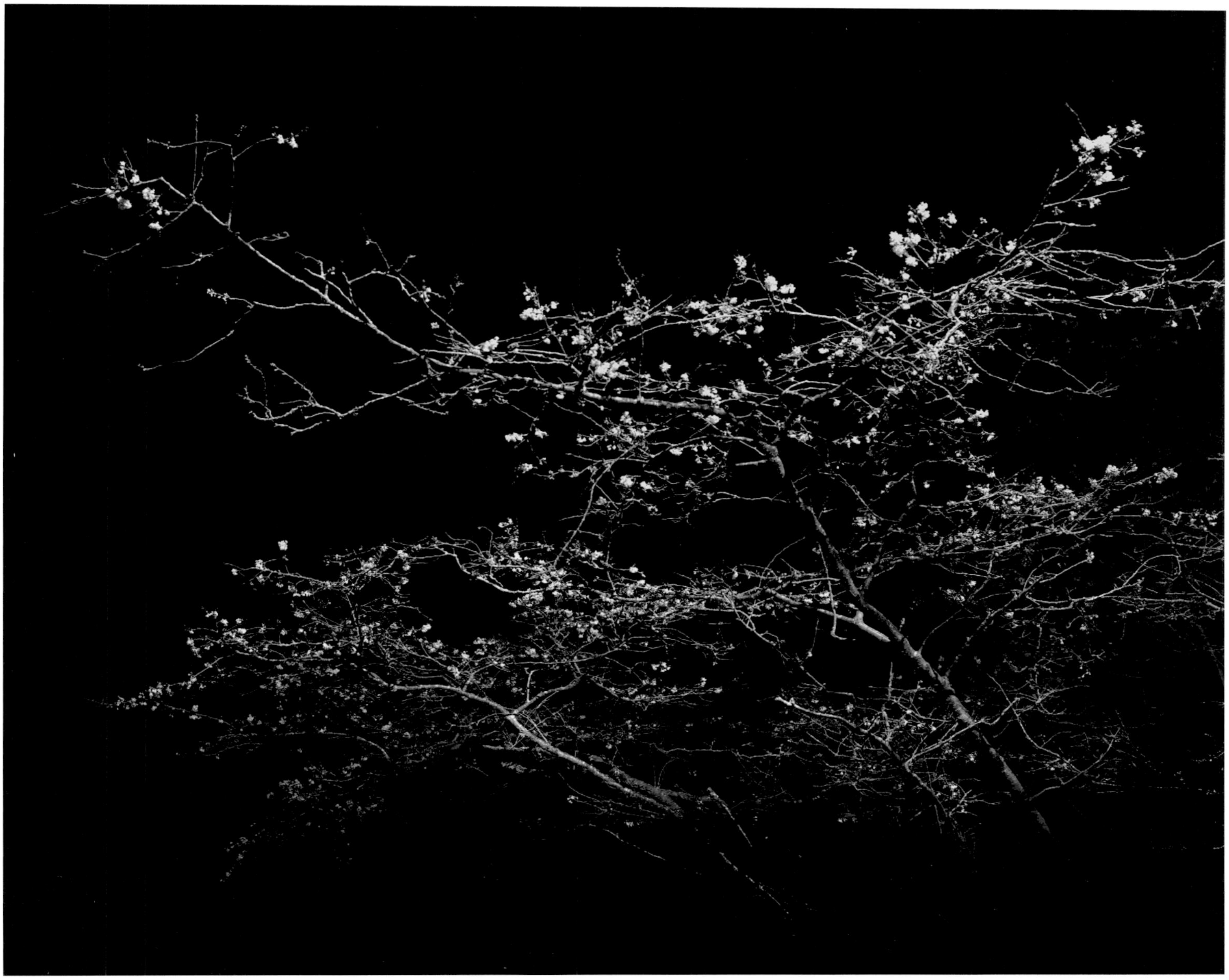

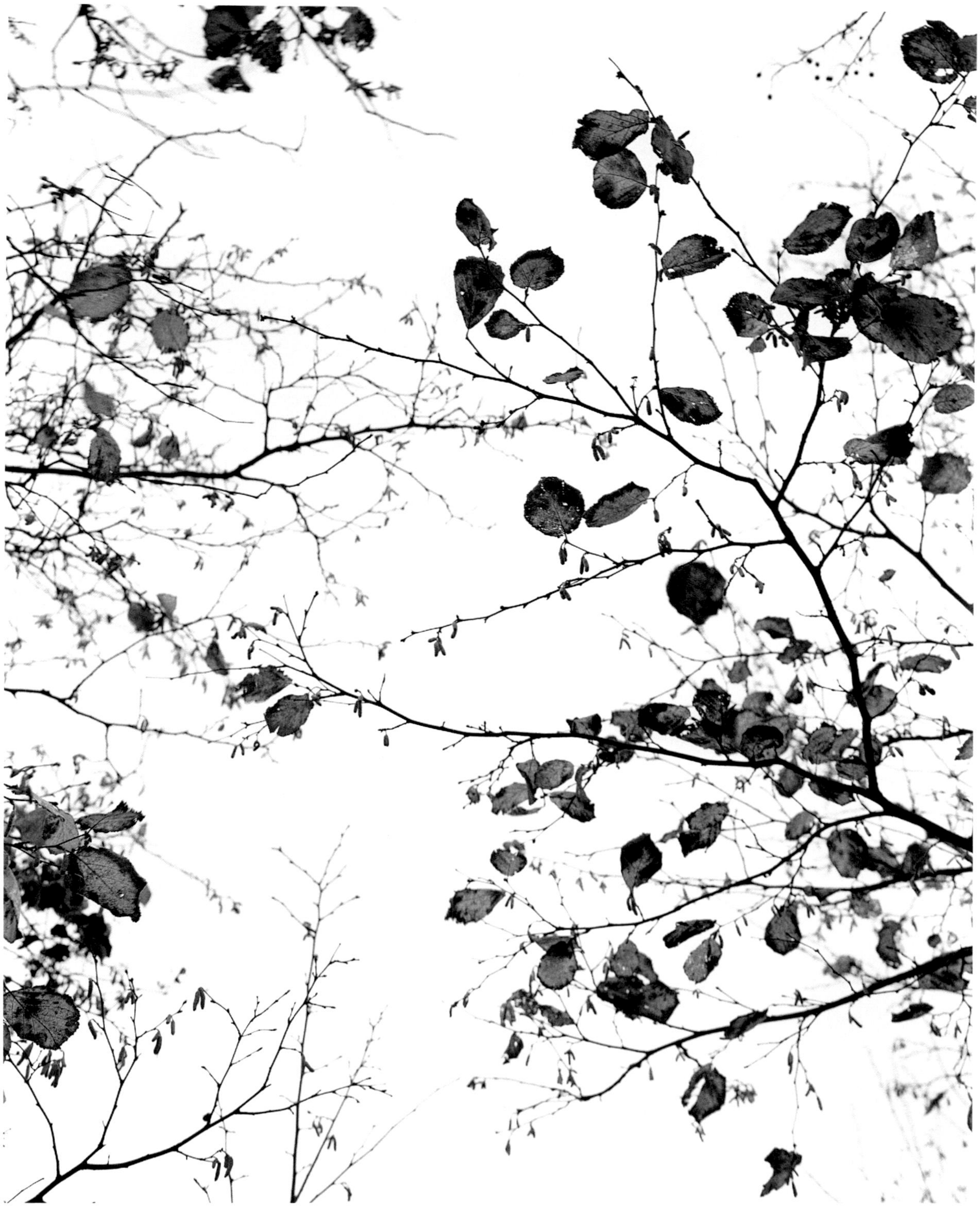

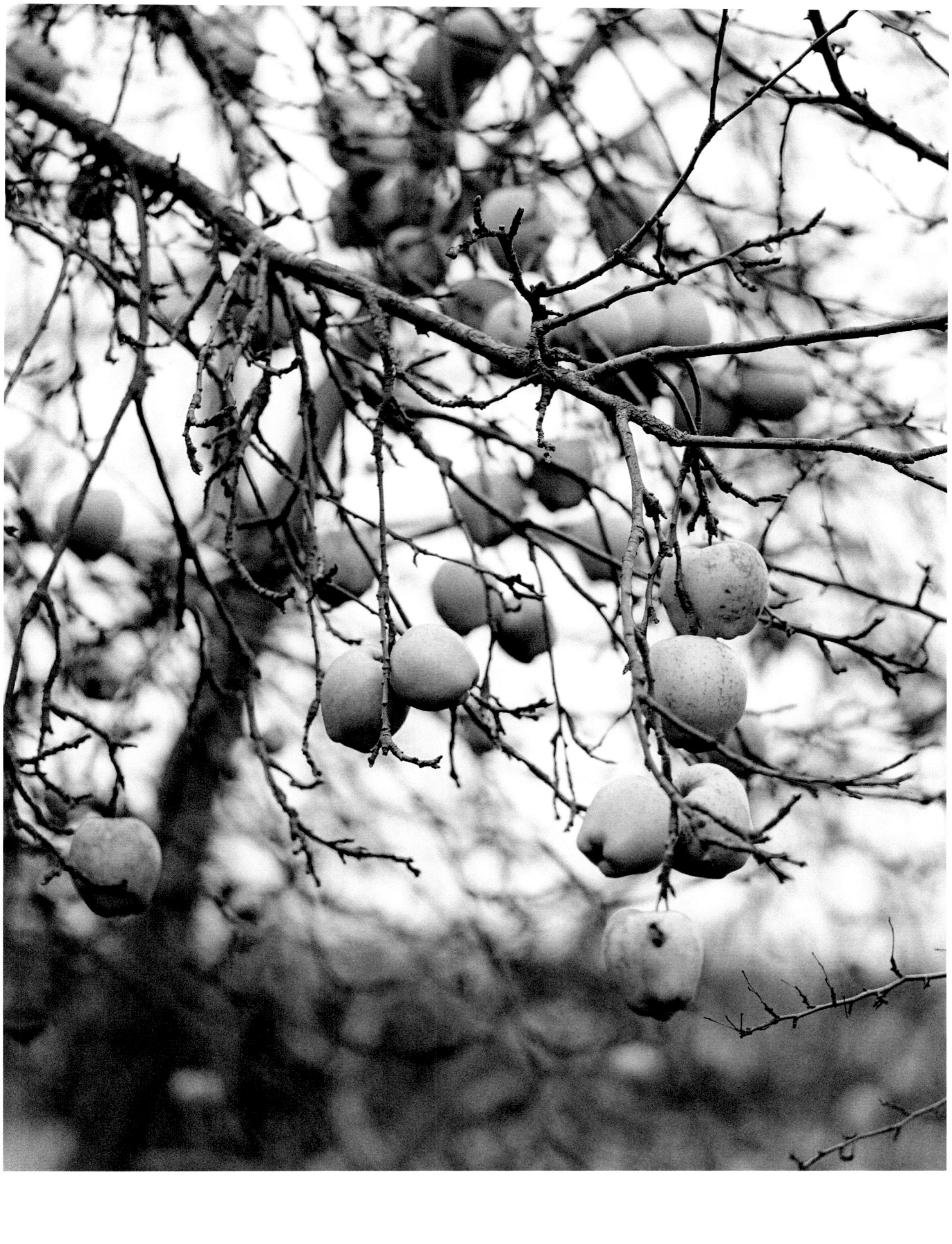

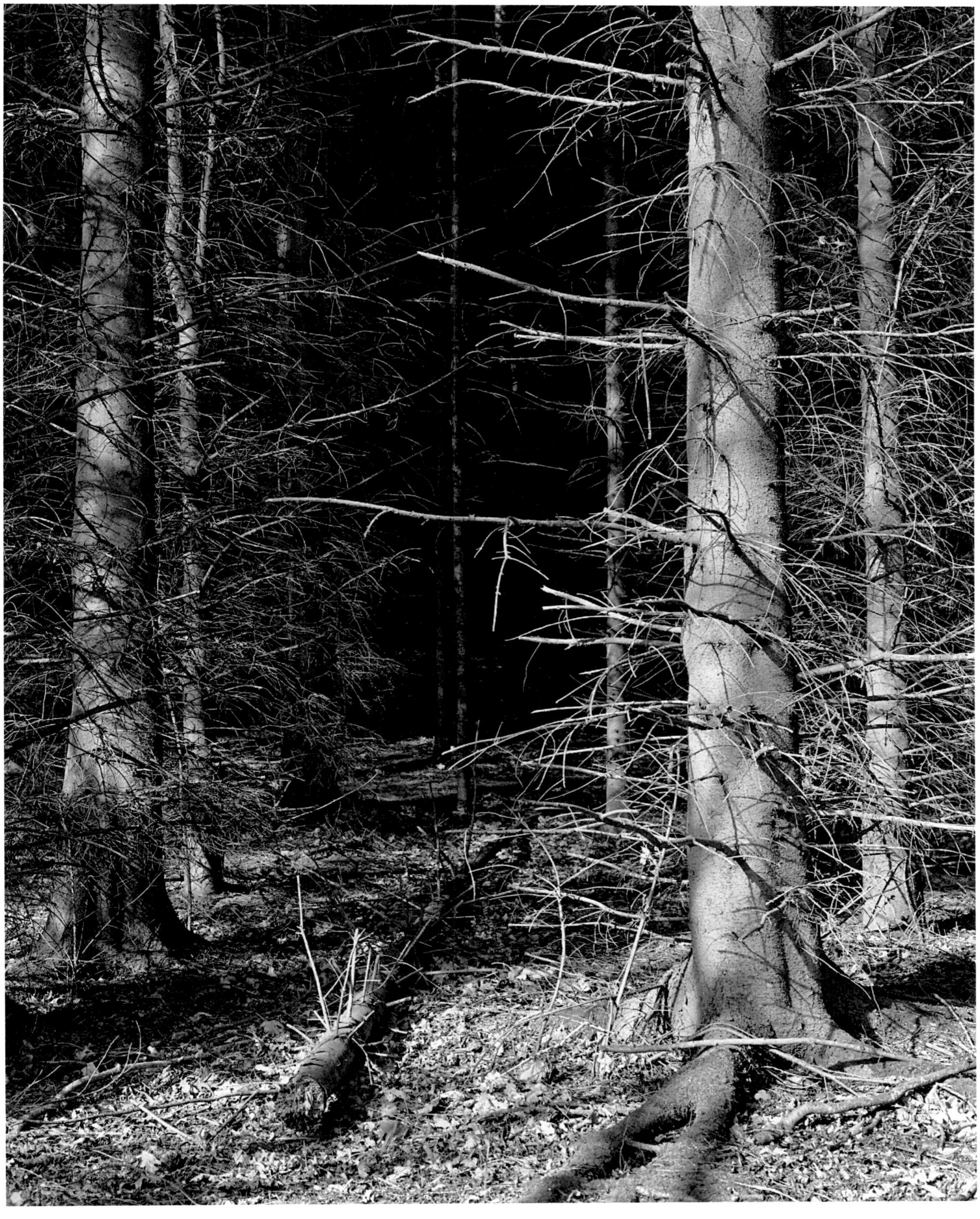

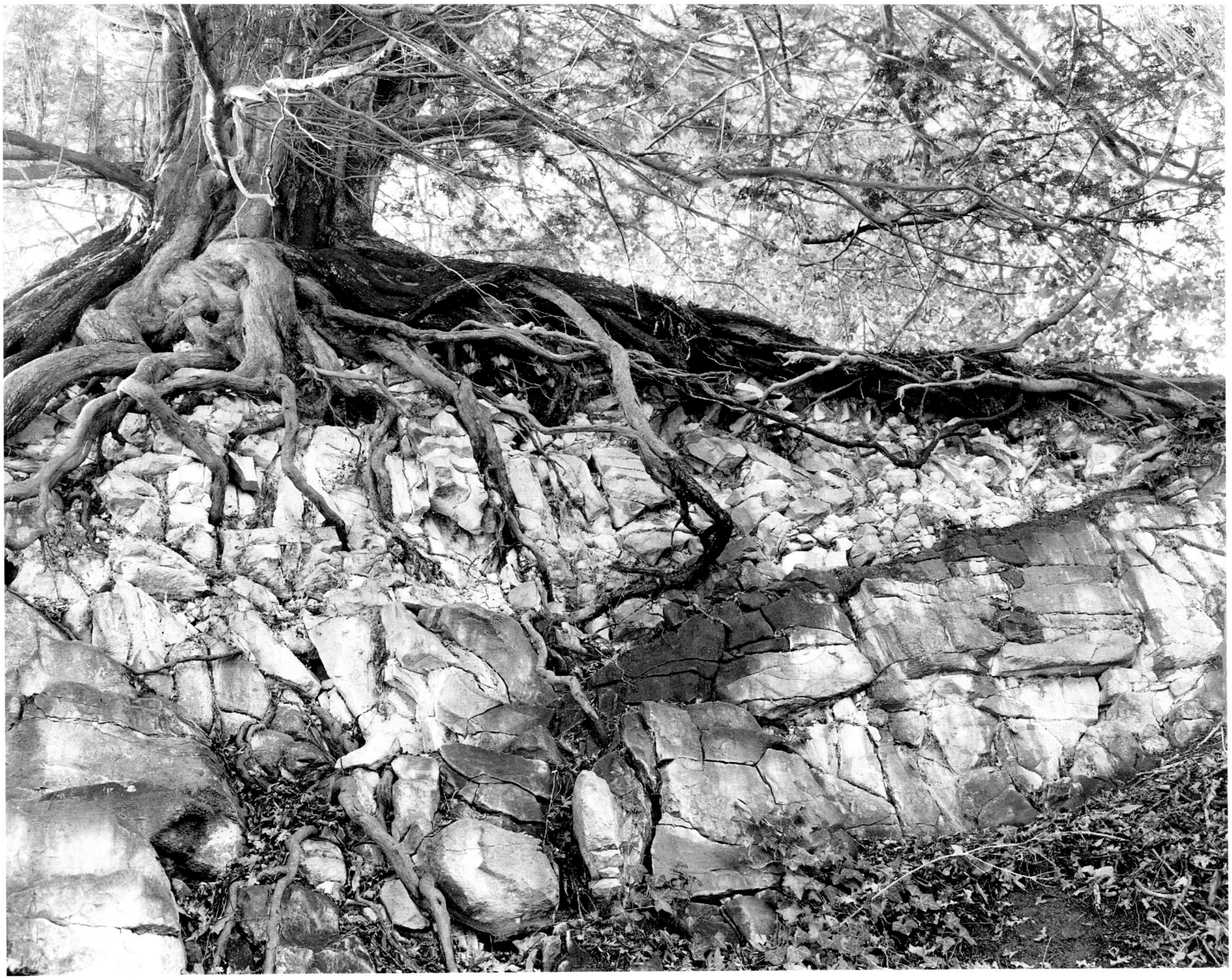

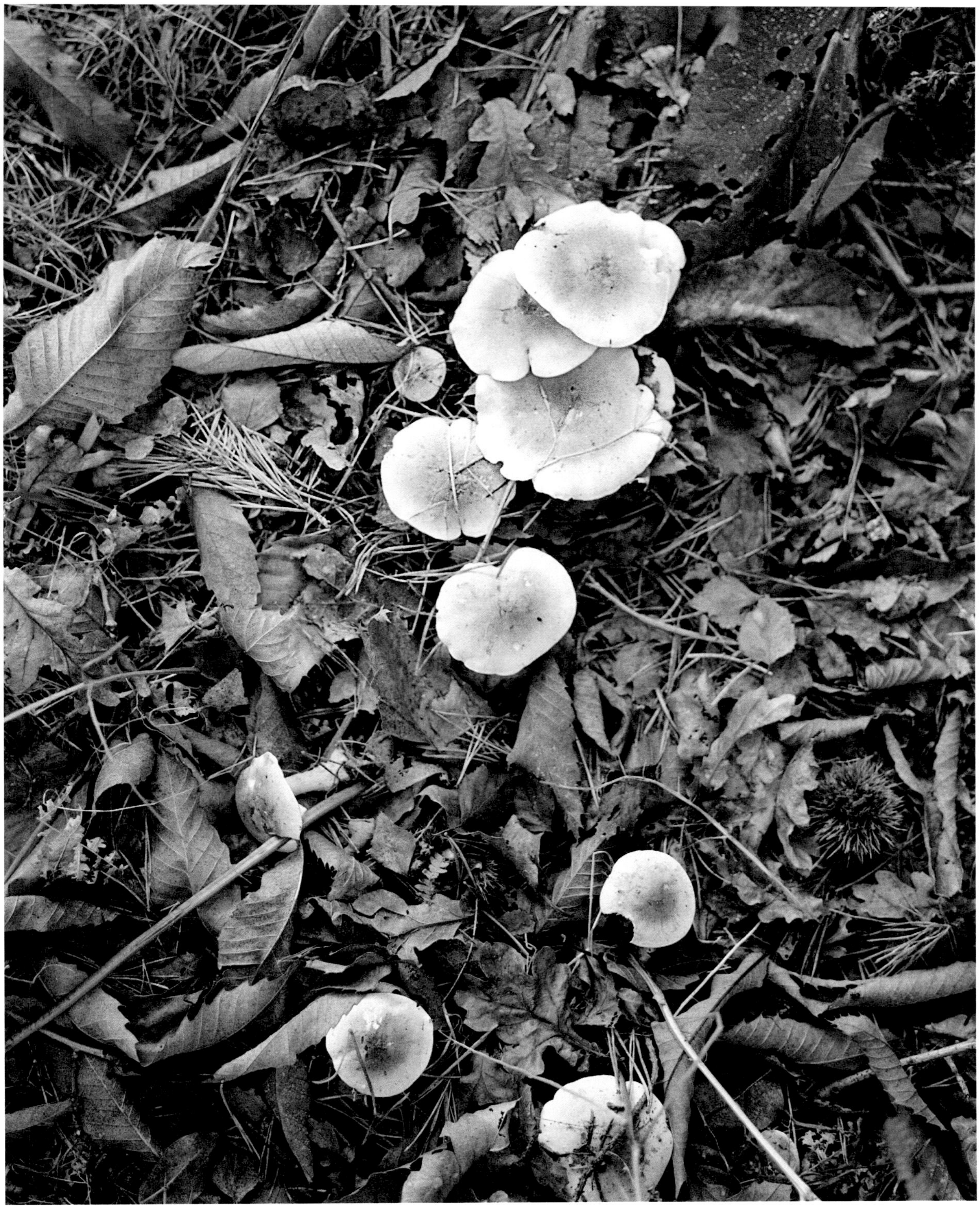

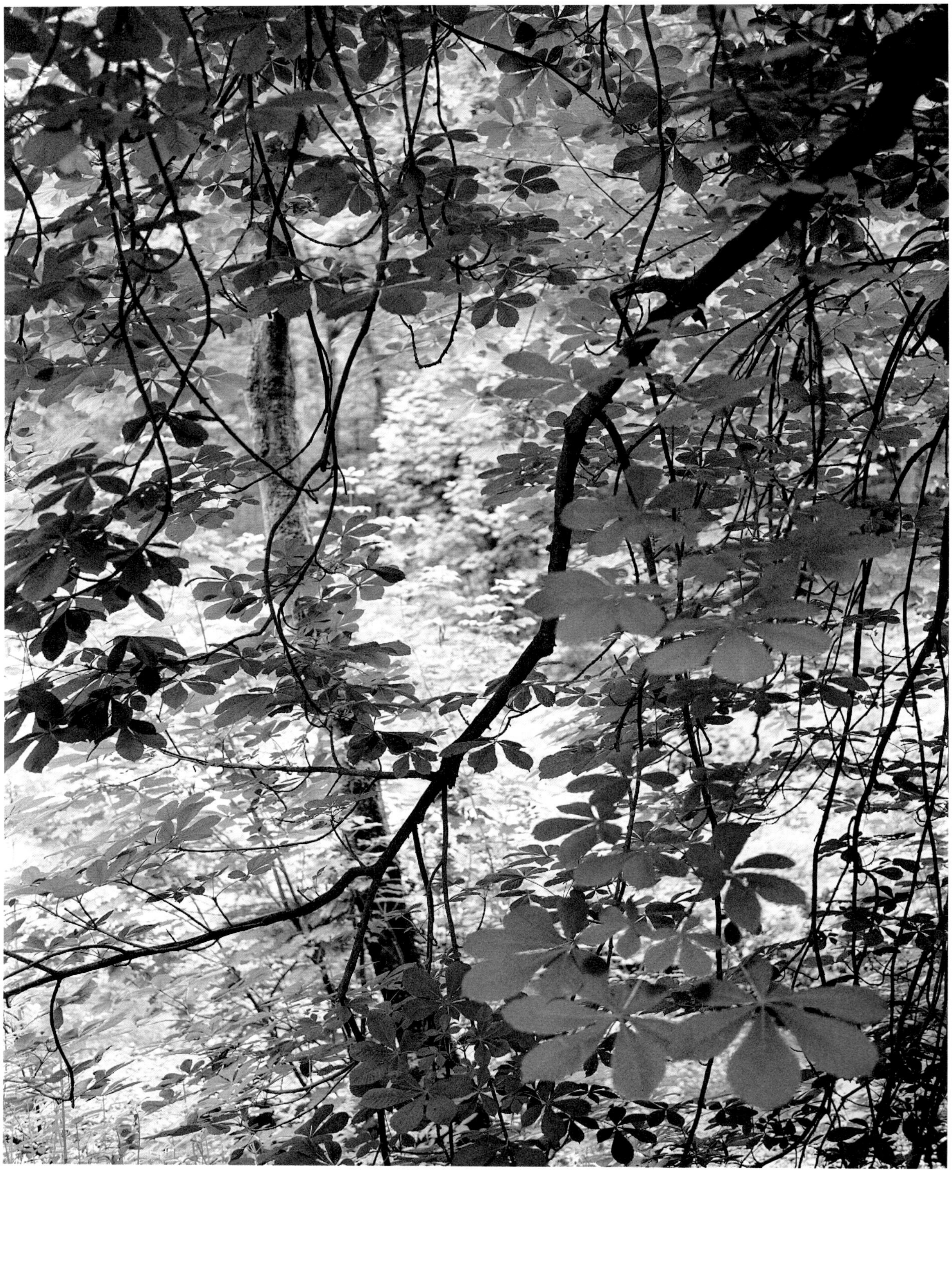

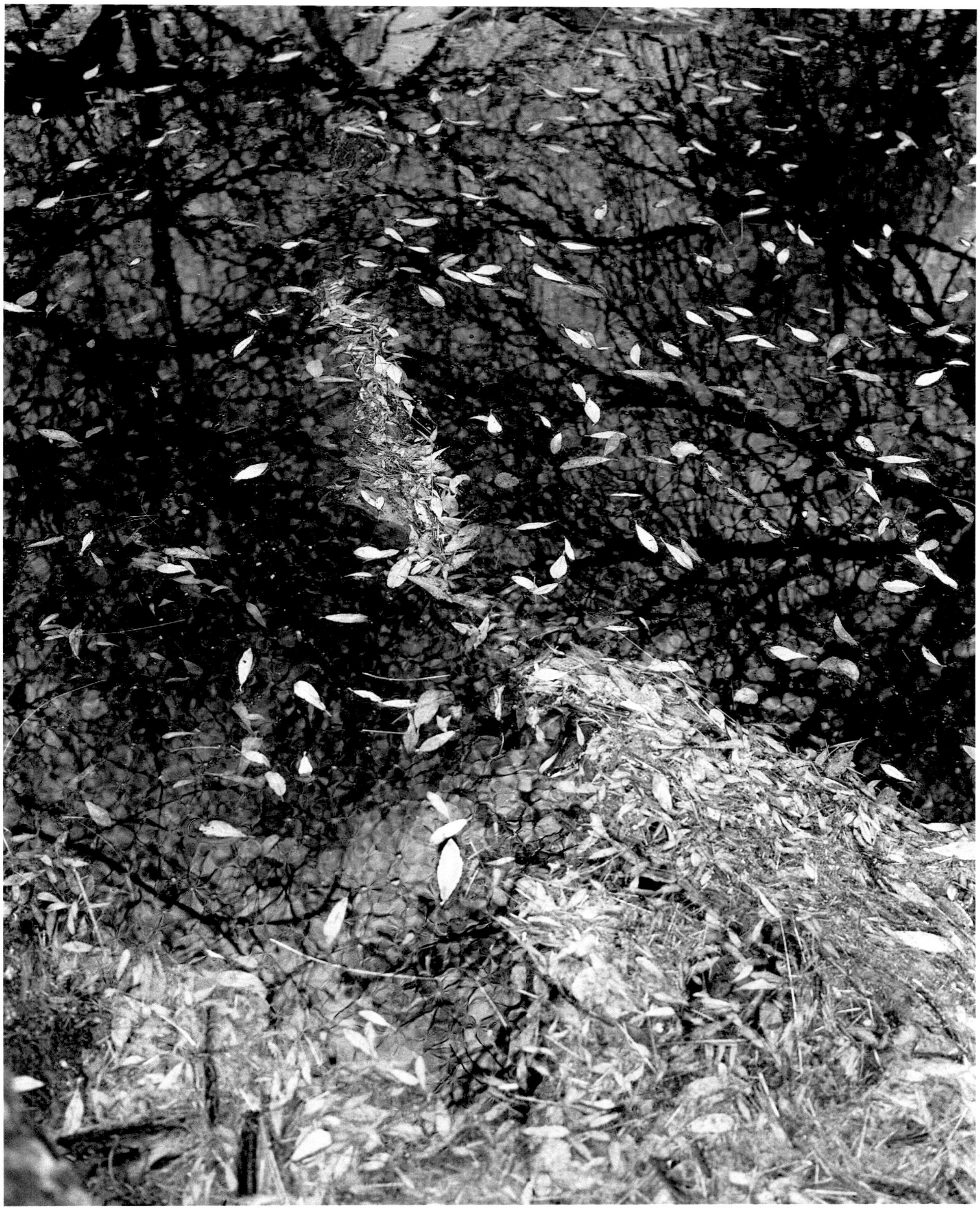

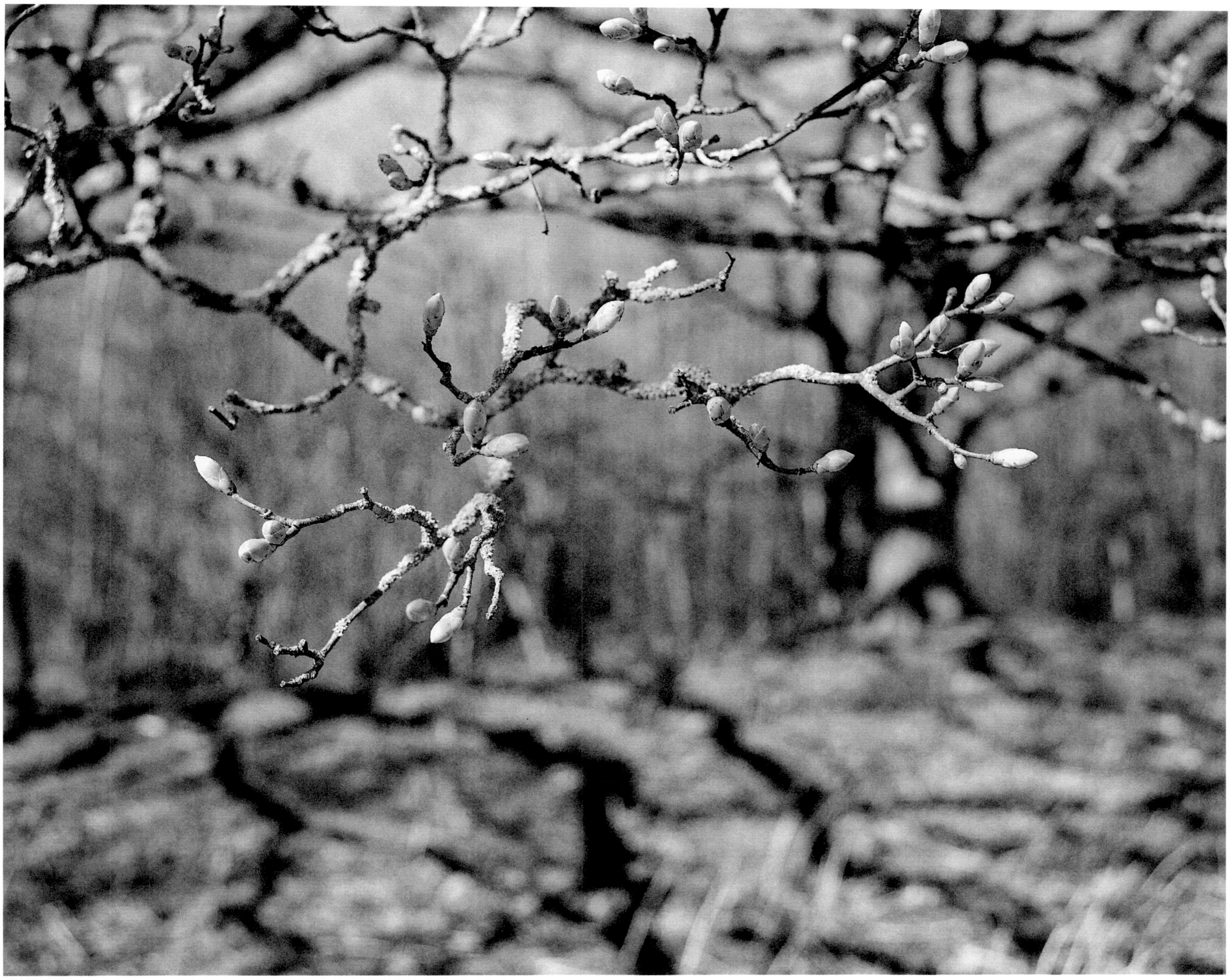

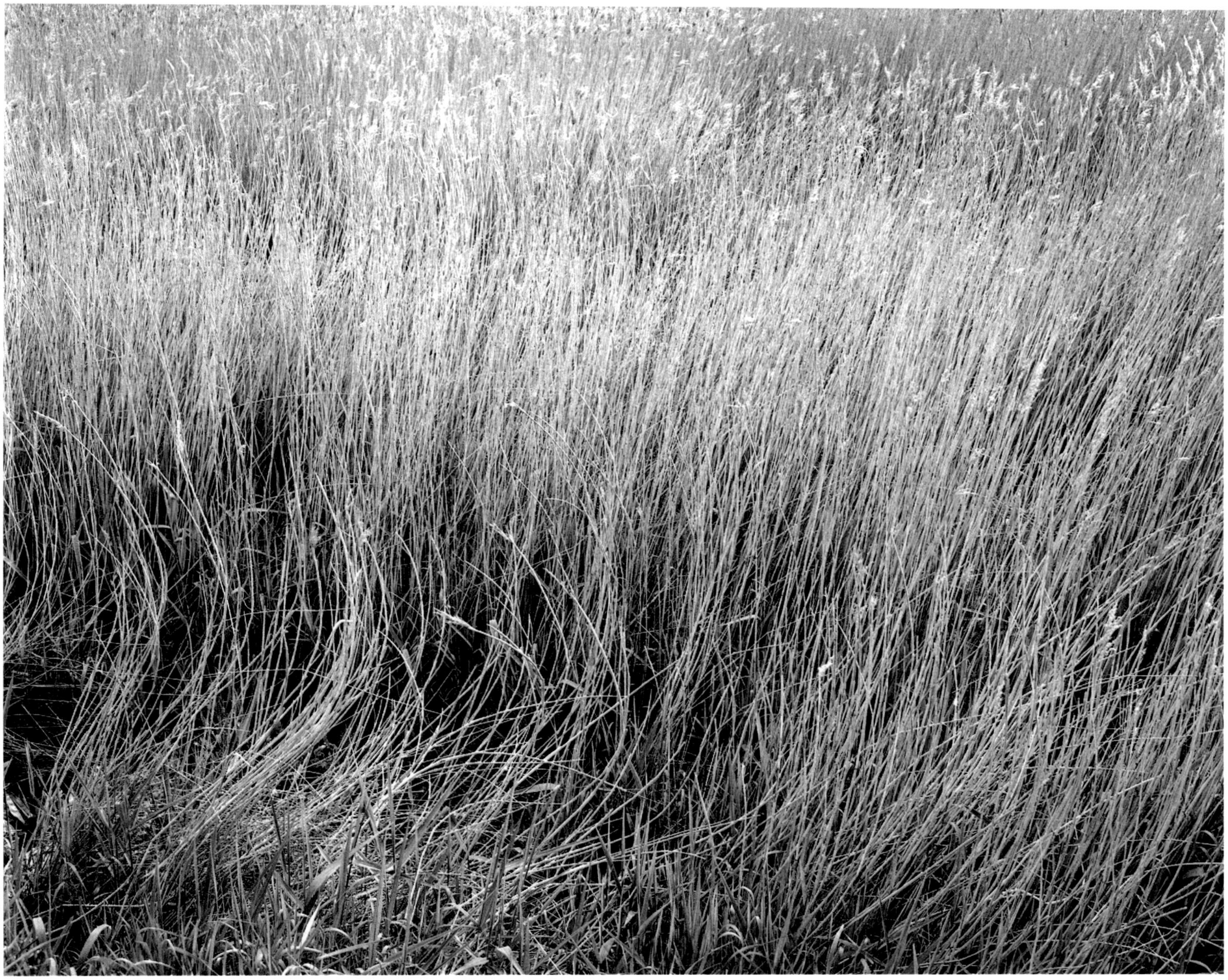

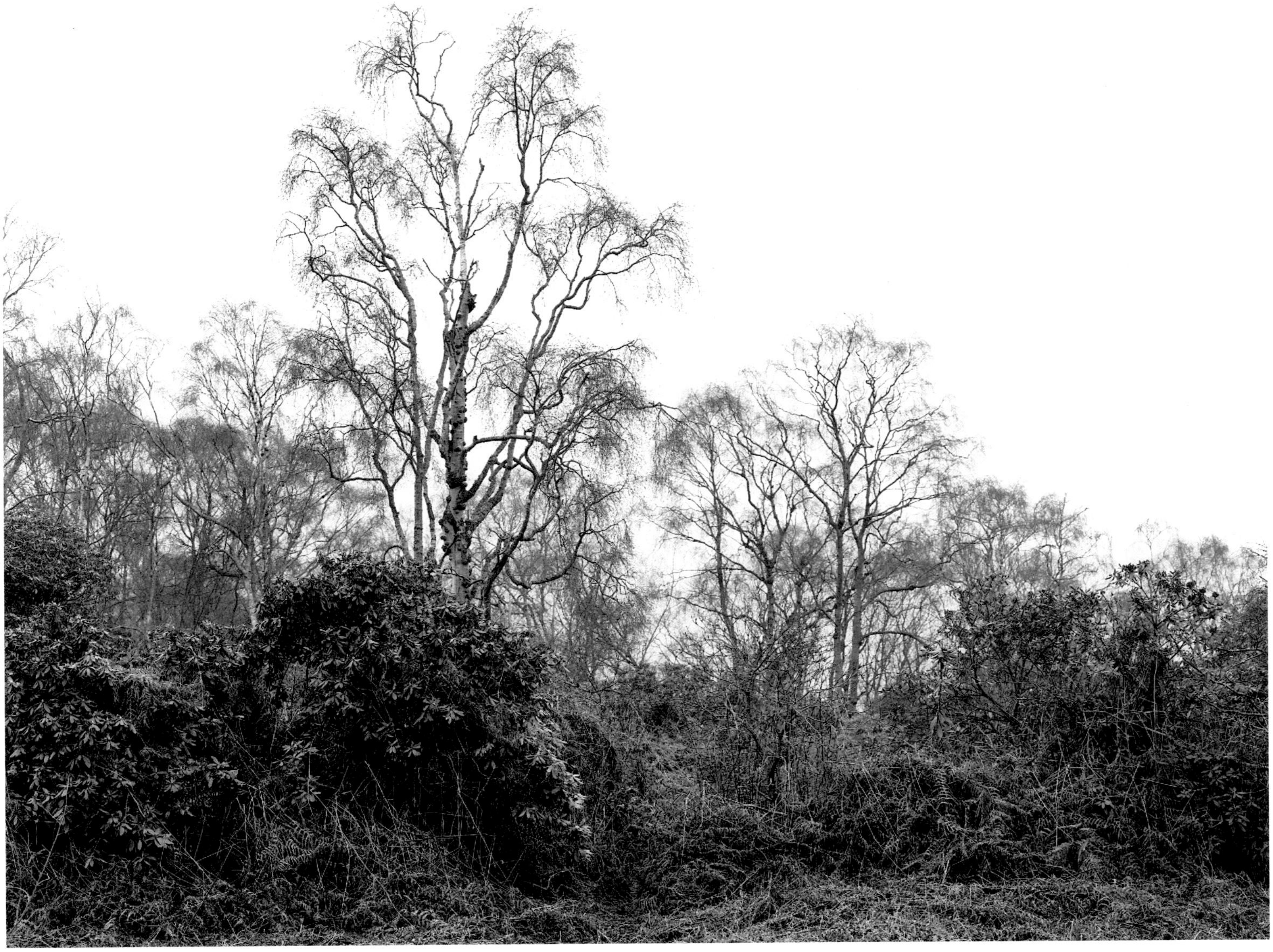

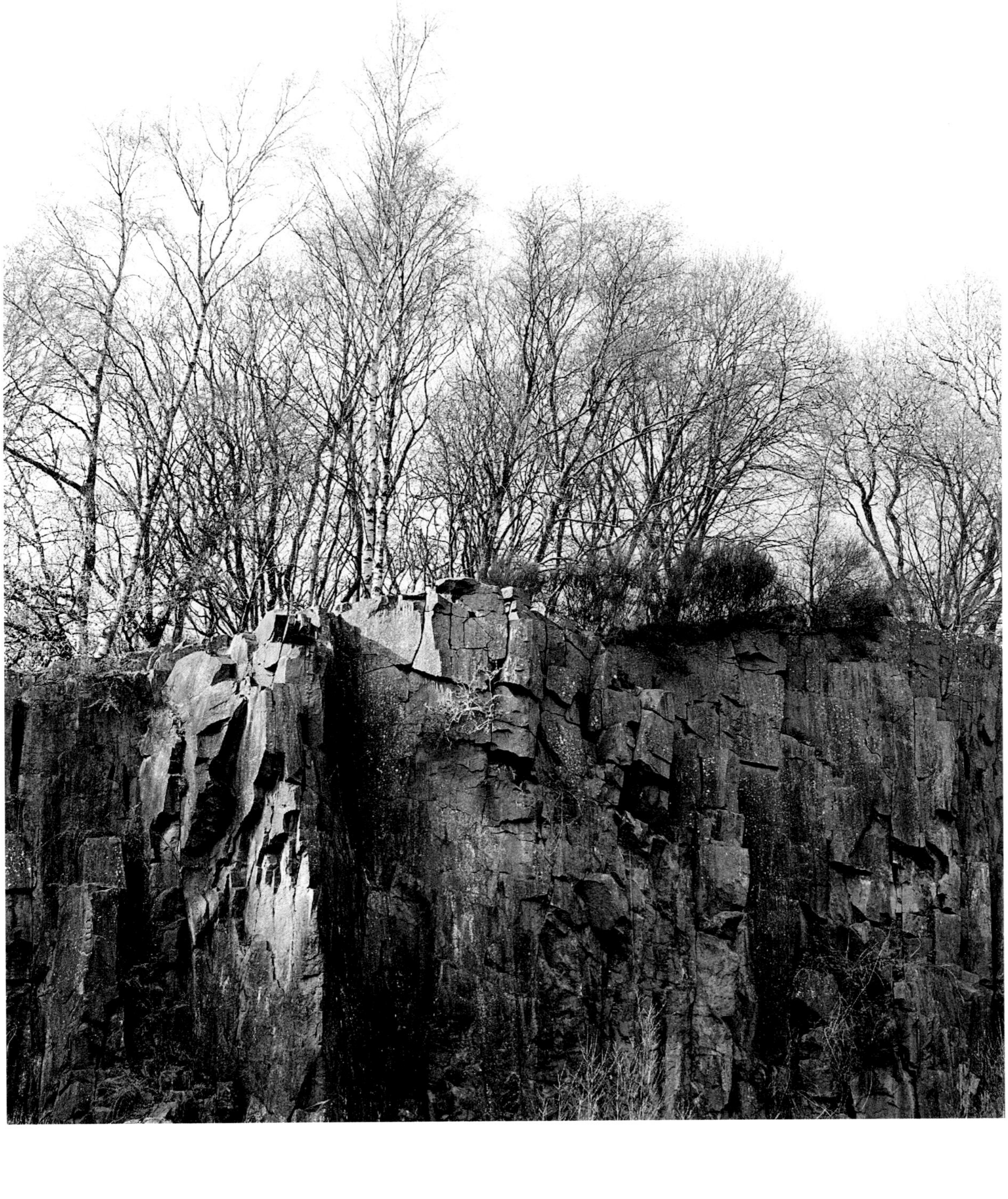

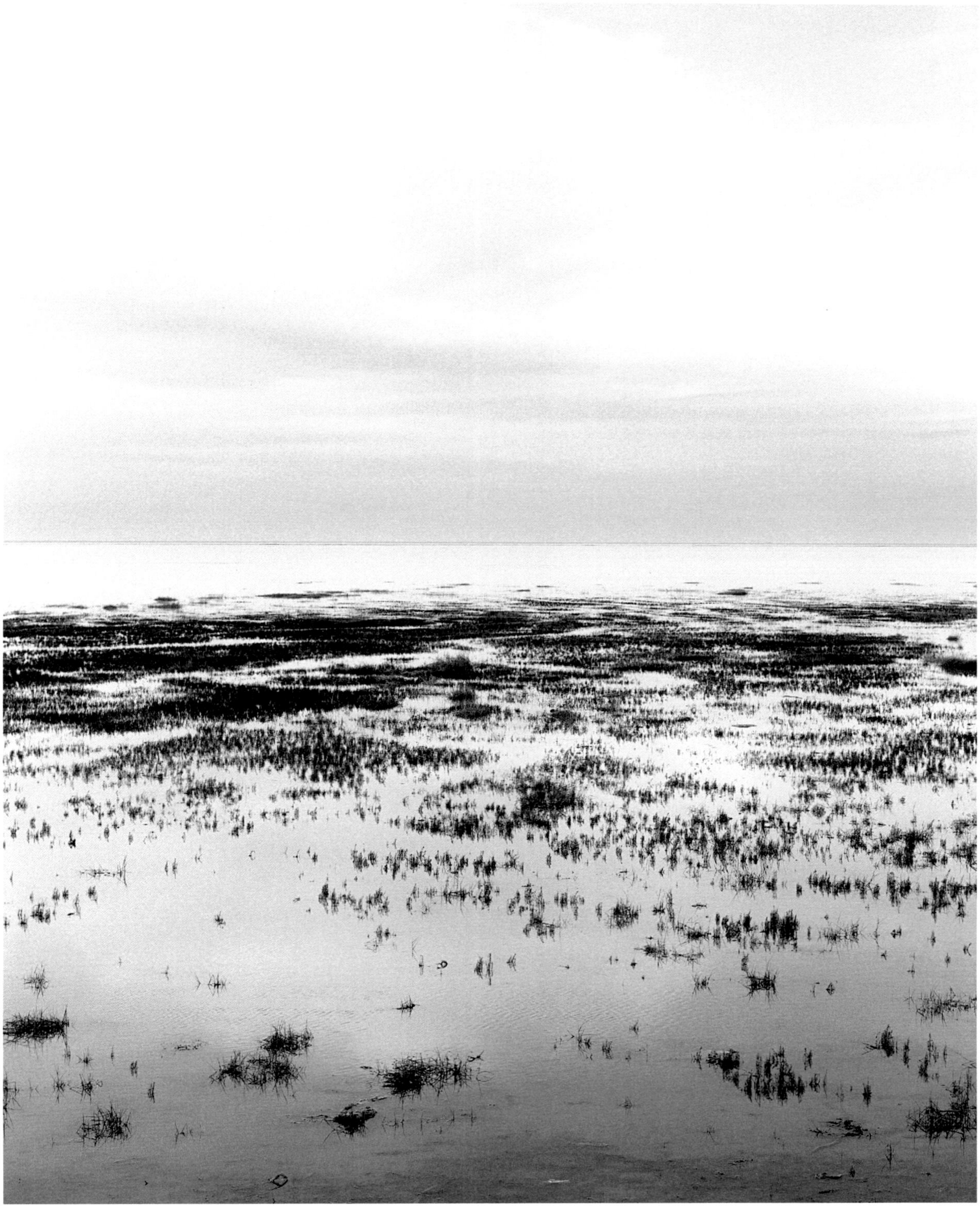

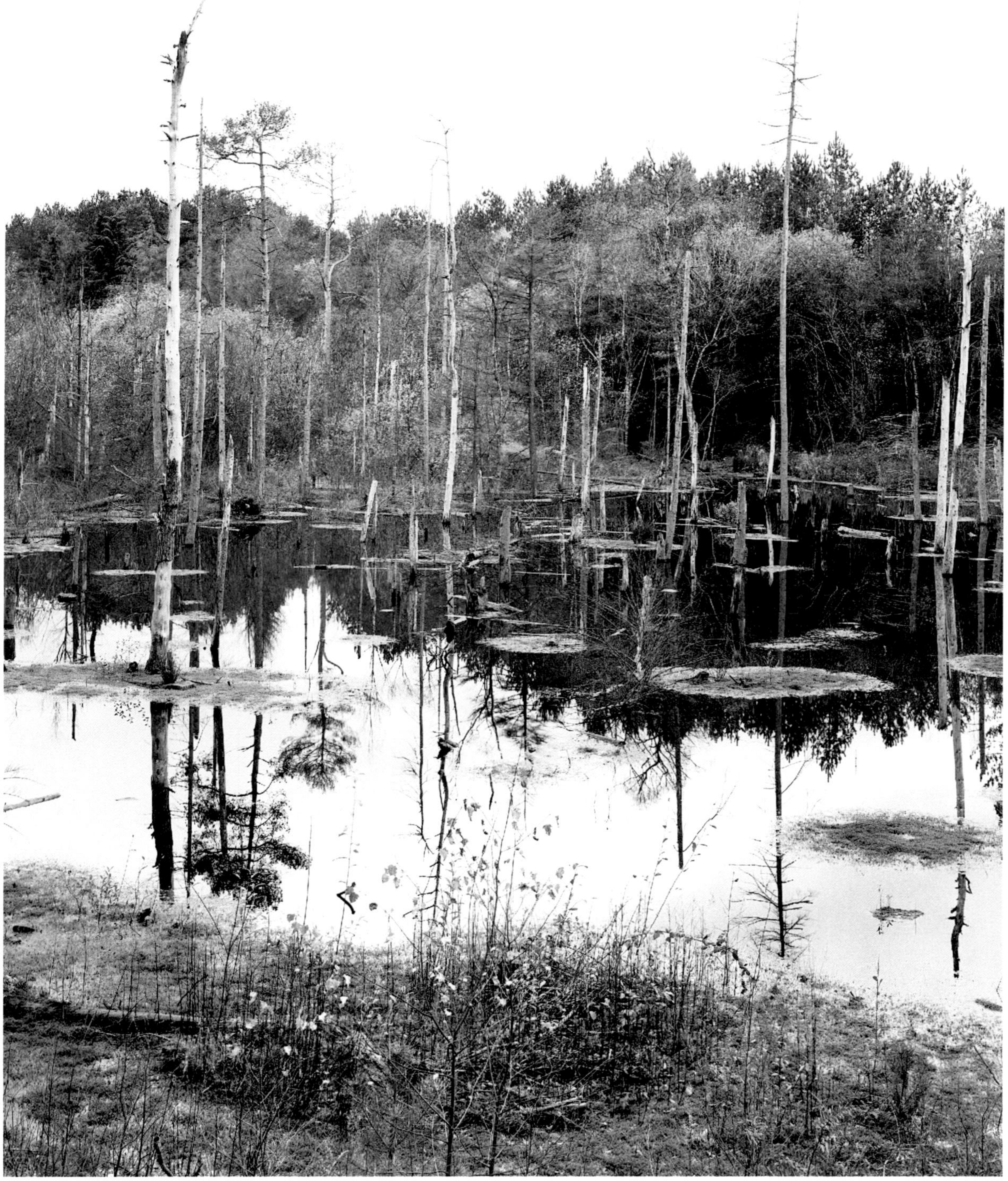

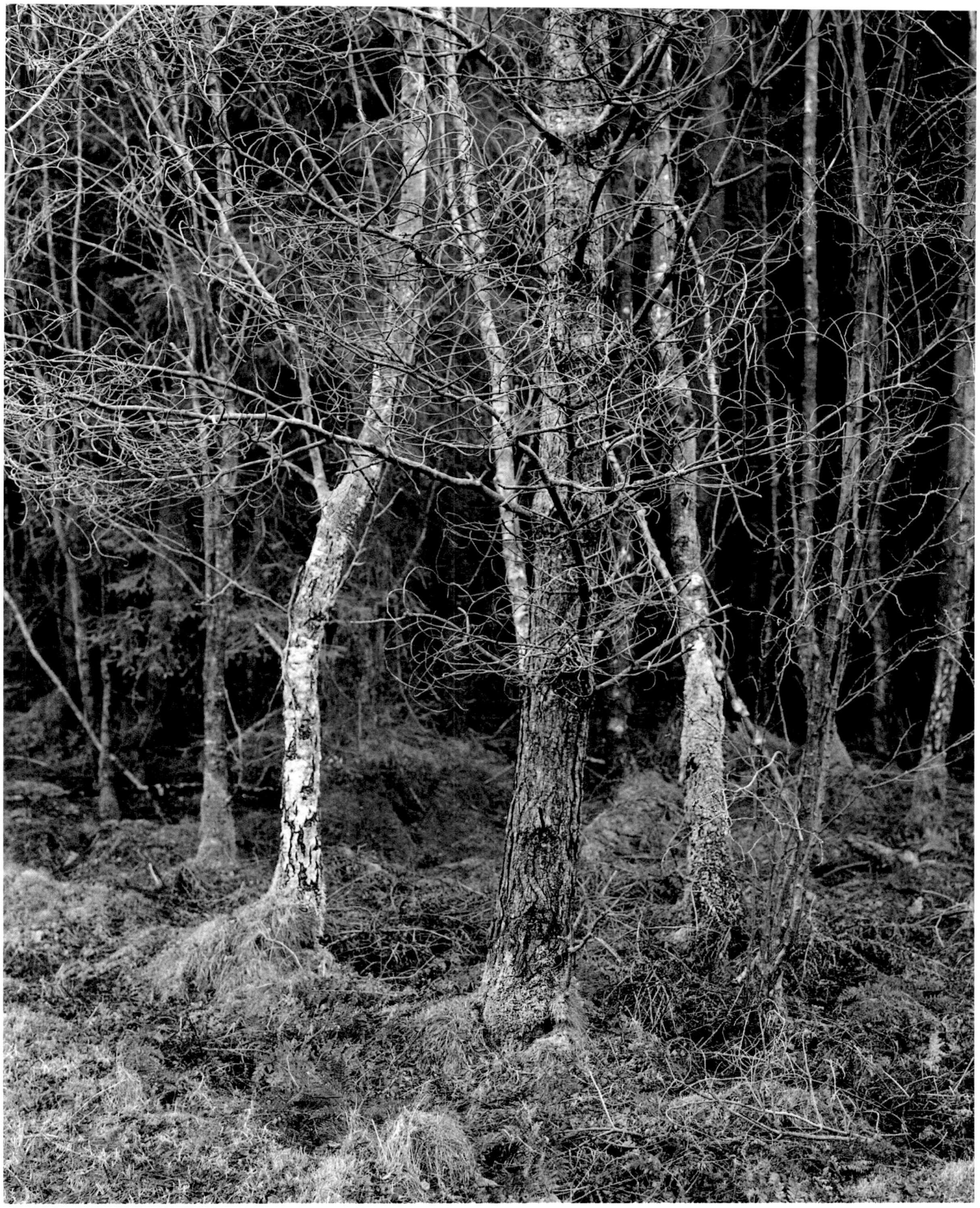

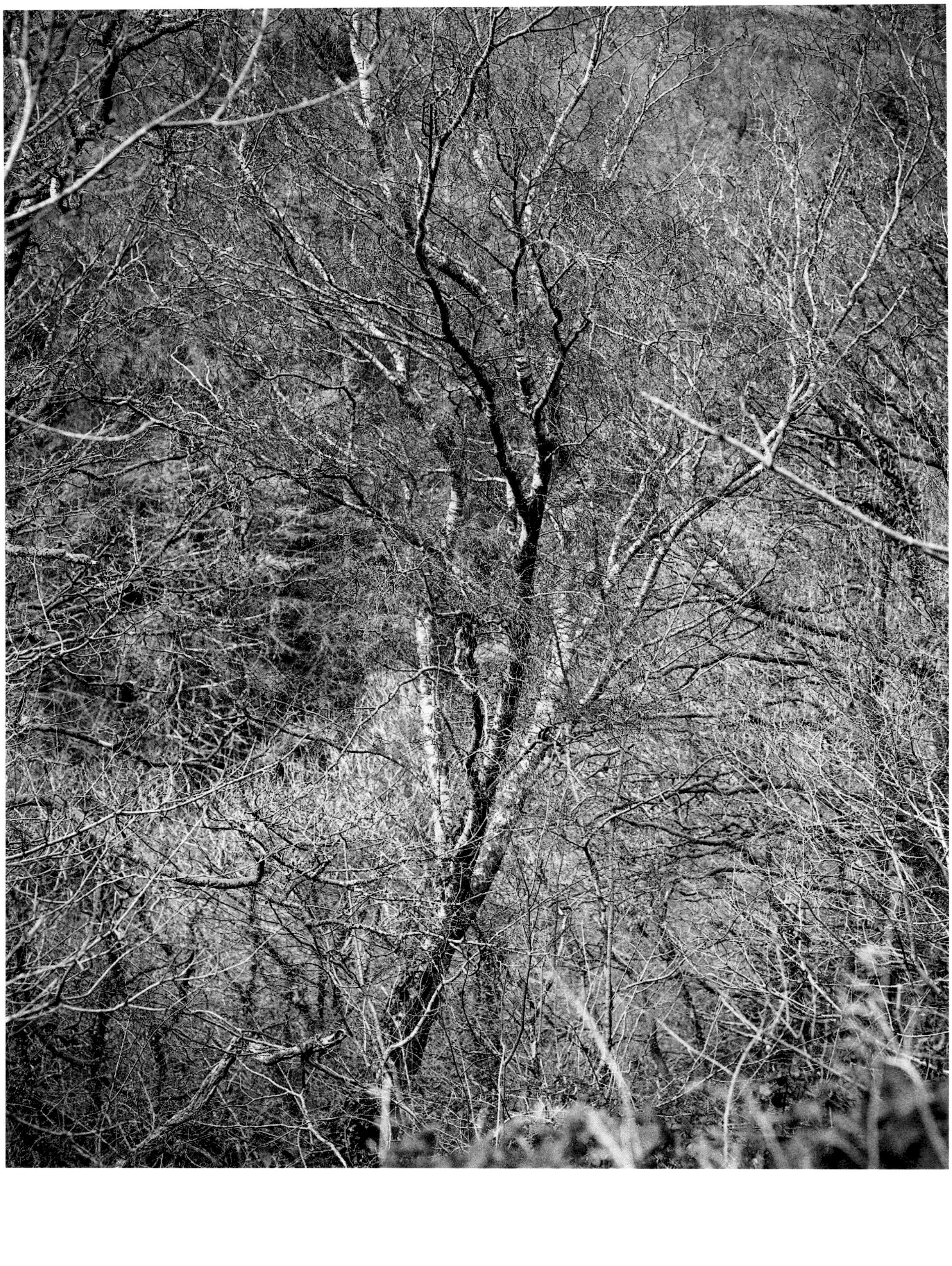

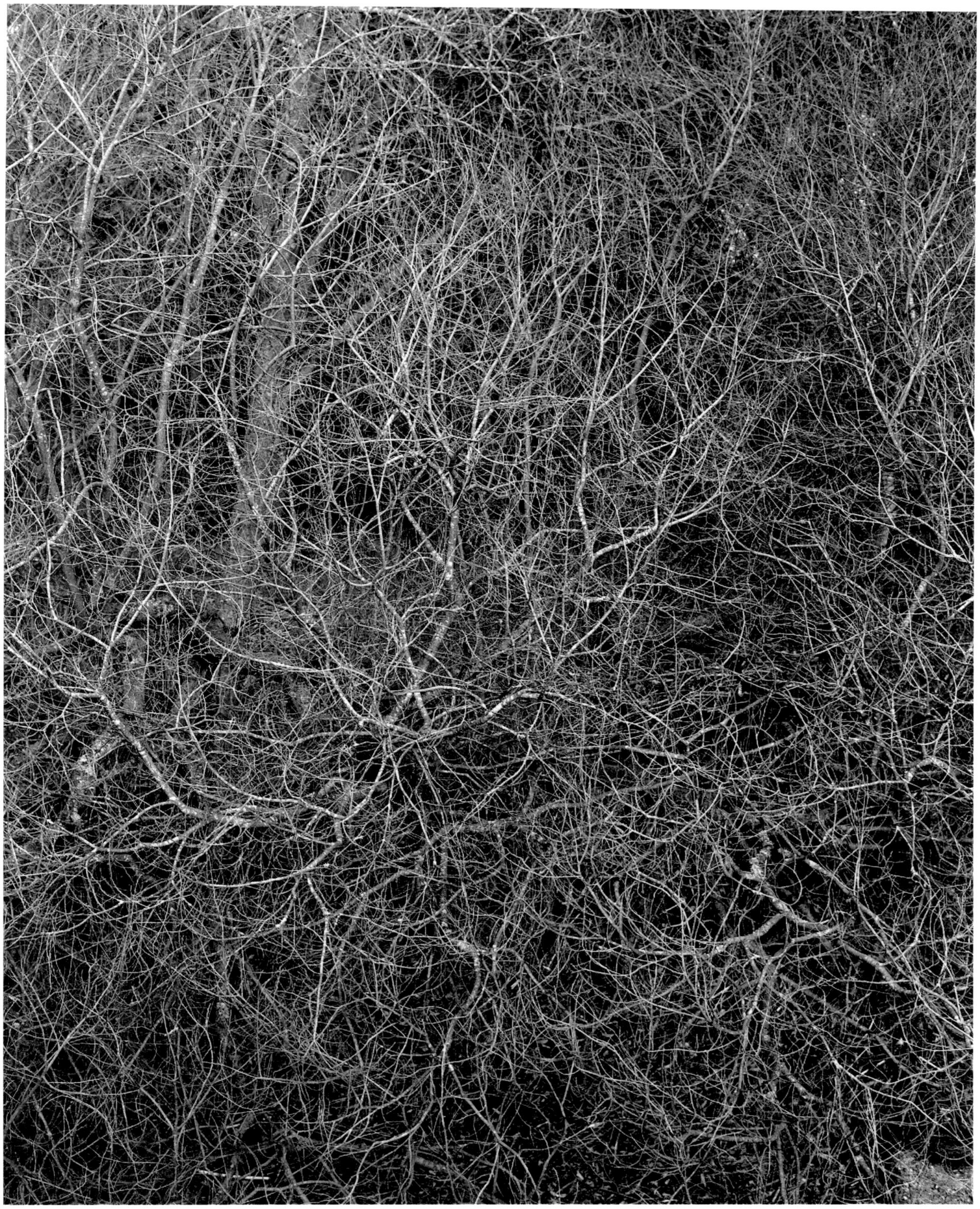

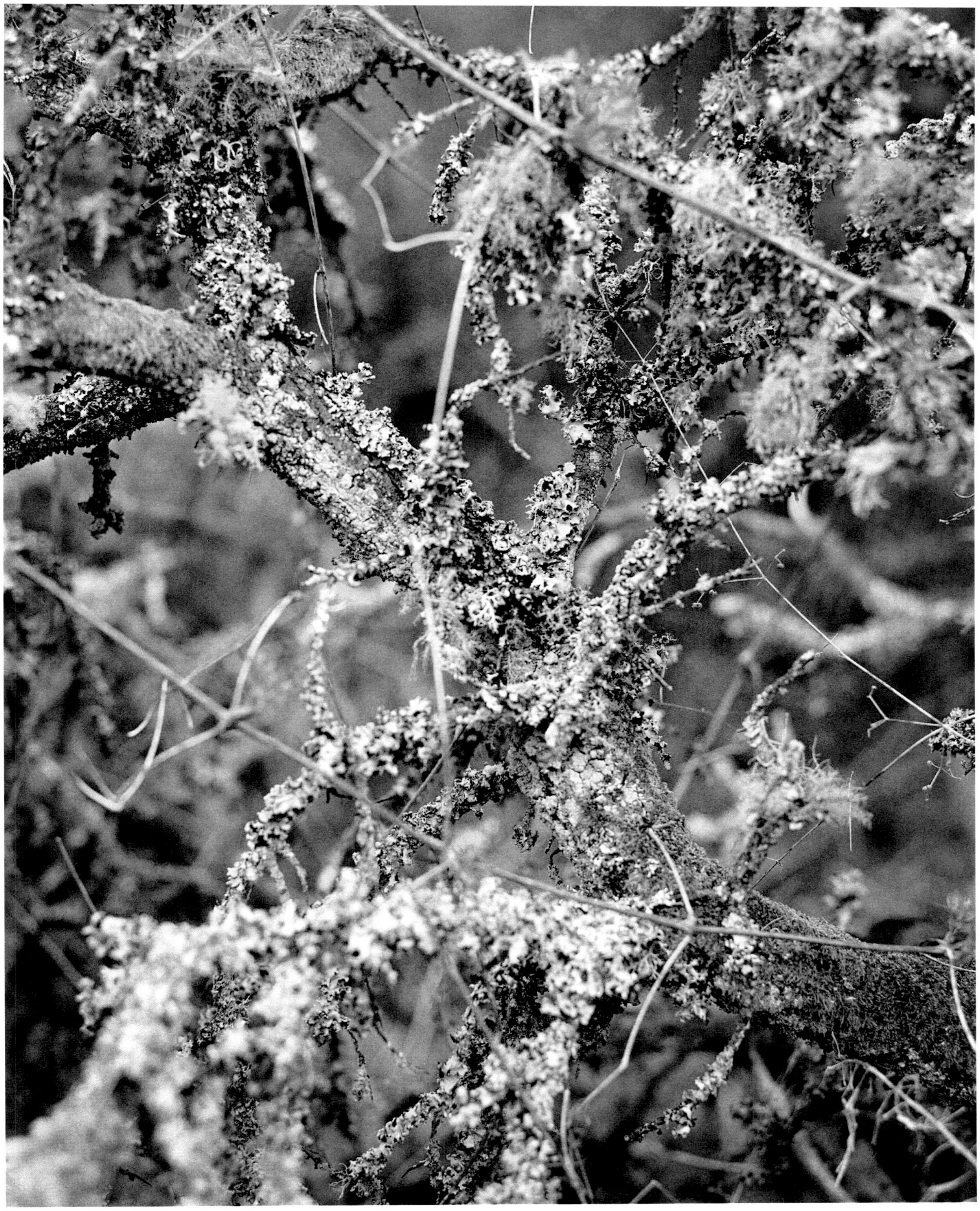

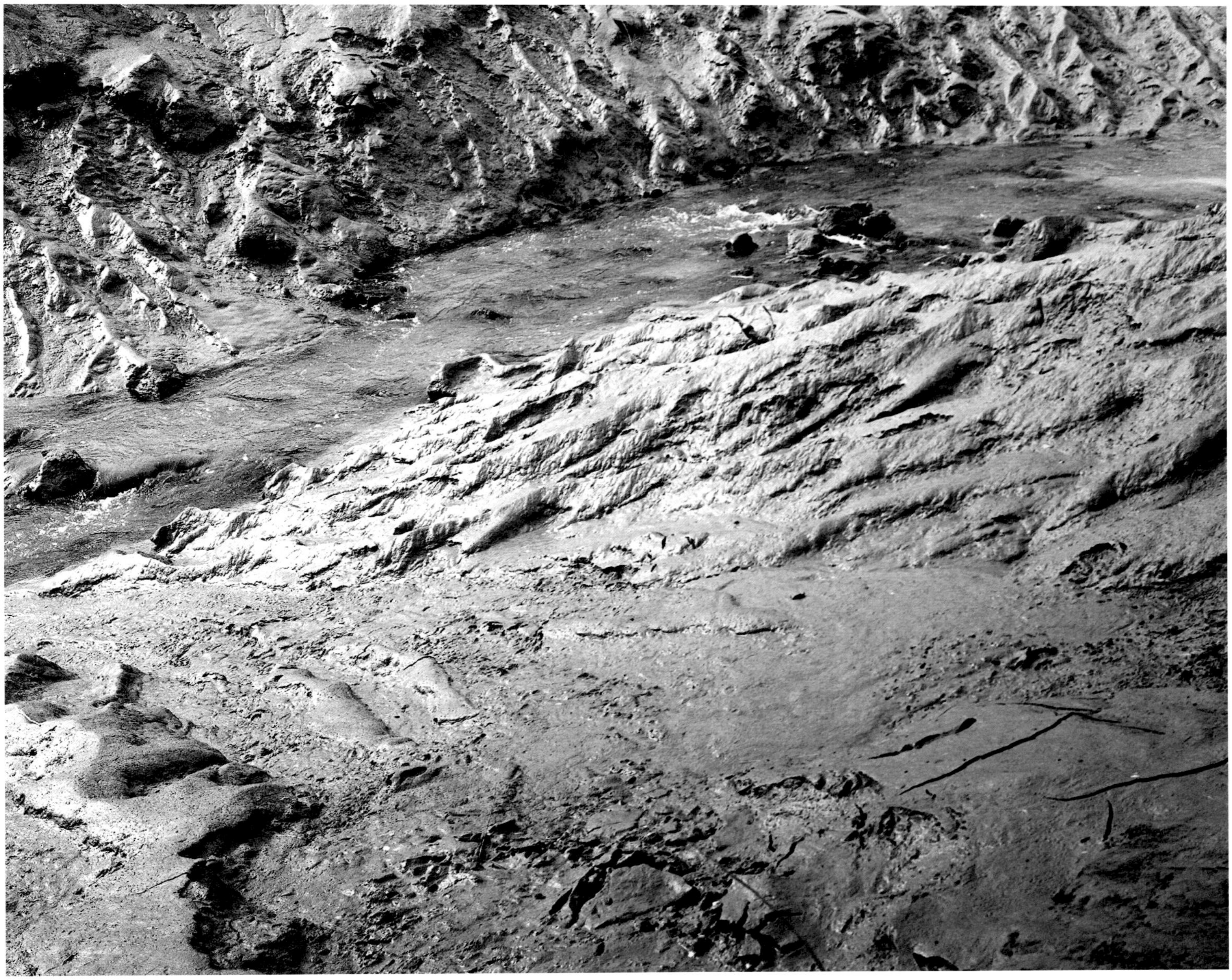

Not Here, Not Anywhere

Helen Baczkowska

The natural gas drilled for in fracking is part of an ancient story; it is a story of rocks older than the British Isles, but it is also a tale of the people whose lives have been shaped by their struggle to stop the drilling for the gas.

The rocks containing the gas are sedimentary shales, formed from older stone weathered and washed into oceans, lakes or swamps; the silt and clay drifted down to a patchy, irregular settling over thousands of years, trapping gases in the faults or flaws and the hollows. Millennia of slumbering followed, sediment compressed by the sediment above, the weight causing lithification, the alchemy of soft deposits turning to rock. Shales can span many ages: north of York and in southern Scotland they are Carboniferous, around three hundred million years old, the same age as most coal seams. These seams too hold natural gas, once a danger to colliers, but now also sought out and drilled. In Sussex, the shales of the Weald date from the Jurassic, around one hundred and fifty million years ago; a time when Stegosaur and Diplodocus moved through forests of ferns, while warm seas spiralled with ammonites.

'Fracking' is a word condensed from 'hydraulic fracturing,' a process in which shale rock is splintered by liquid, usually water thickened with chemical agents, injected under high pressure. Grains of silica sand or aluminium oxide, proppants to the industry, hold the cracks open when the pressure is relieved, allowing the release of the trapped natural gas to a surface wellhead. Fracking is one of several 'unconventional' methods of gas extraction techniques developed to reach inaccessible reserves and although carried out on a small scale in the UK since the 1970s, the proposals to develop these unconventional methods on an industrial scale were at the heart of concerns raised across the UK in the early twenty-first century.

For many communities, encounters with fracking started with seismic surveys of shales, where sound waves bounced off underground rock form detailed images of local geology and locate hidden reservoirs of gas. The mapping out of license blocks, delineating areas suitable for fracking, followed, along with submissions of planning applications for drill sites and haulage roads. As the planning applications began, so too did the voices of dissent, growing louder into demonstrations and objections to planning decisions, to protest camps and direct action.

As I listen to recordings of interviews with campaigners, recorded by John Volynchook, I hear heartbeats of my own past, entwined as it is with the history of environmental resistance in Britain. Over twenty-five years ago, in the south of England, I watched a hill called Twyford Down destroyed to make way for a motorway. The Down was one of the most protected landscapes in England, designated for its flower-rich grassland, ancient monuments and breath-taking beauty, yet, over two years, tonne after tonne of chalk was gouged out and spread on the water meadows below, levelling the land for the carriageways. Despite the loss of Twyford Down, the protests there gave rise to a confident and radical environmental movement, which had to swiftly learn the language of campaigning and the phrases of the planning process. When we lived on the land and took direct action against the motorway construction, we acquired the vocabulary of squatting law and eviction, of arrest and injunction, bail and imprisonment.

Fracking started to attract public attention when seismic surveys began in 2010, with the northwest of England becoming a focal point for growing unease with the industry. License blocks here stretch northwards from Merseyside to Blackpool, along a coastline of towns, such as Formby, Southport and Lytham St Annes, with beaches, sand dunes and salt marsh ebbing into the Irish Sea. The blocks reach inland along the rivers Ribble, Alt and Wyre and eastwards across the Lancashire Plain towards the Pennines, the high rocky backbone of north England.

As more surveys and applications for fracking came forward, opposition groups were established in communities across the UK, from central Scotland to England's south coast. These were frequently founded by a handful of people sharing their concerns; some became social media platforms for sharing news, whilst others went on to hold public meetings to share information and generate ideas for opposing the applications. Some groups developed links with the local press and worked up detailed, informed objections to the plans, sometimes raising thousands of pounds to mount a legal challenge. By 2014, there was a network of groups providing mutual aid and support across the land.

Unease over fracking proposals strengthened an awareness of environmental issues among campaigners: the connection between climate change and the extraction of fossil fuels, the potential contamination of groundwater supplies by unrecovered fracking fluids and the disruption and damage to the property and health of residents living close to well sites. Alongside impacts on climate, on earth and water and air, there is the raw shock of fracked landscapes in the United States, New Zealand and Australia, where aerial photographs of mountains and forests show industrialised grids of new roads and the pale, stripped squares of well sites stretching out across the horizon.

In November 2019, in the run up to the General Election, the UK Government halted fracking in England. The timing of this moratorium, in the wake of unpredictable earth tremors and as competing political parties vied for votes in northern England, led to much conjecture over the motivation behind it and how long it will last. As I write, in spring 2020, a fragile peace still holds, although applications for fracking are still being submitted—the outcomes and consequences of fracking in the UK still to unfold.

Plate	Licence Block	Licence Area
01	SZ58a	South
02	SD31	North-West
03	NS98b	Scotland
04	SD44	North-West
05	SK57c	North
06	SS87a	Wales
07	SN80	Wales
08	SS89	Wales
09	SK96	North
10	SD43b	North-West
11	SD52	North-West
12	SE68a	North-East
13	SK67a	North
14	SK57c	North
15	SD60	North-West
16	TA14	North-East
17	SN80	Wales
18	SU91a	South-East
19	SU90a	South-East
20	SK66b	North
21	SJ56	North-West
22	SE75	North-East
23	SD52	North-West
24	SD31	North-West
25	SJ69	North-West
26	SU90a	South-East
27	SY97	South
28	SK73	North
29	SJ28	North-West
30	SJ66	North-West
31	SY98c	South
32	SE50b	North
33	NS99a	Scotland
34	SU91a	South-East
35	TQ14b	South-East
36	SD60d	North-West
37	SZ8a	South
38	SE67	North-East
39	ST24	South-West
40	SD30	North-West
41	NS77	Scotland
42	SD31	North-West
43	SJ57	North-West
44	SE98	North-East
45	SS89	Wales
46	SD71	North-West
47	SS87a	Wales
48	ST24	South-West

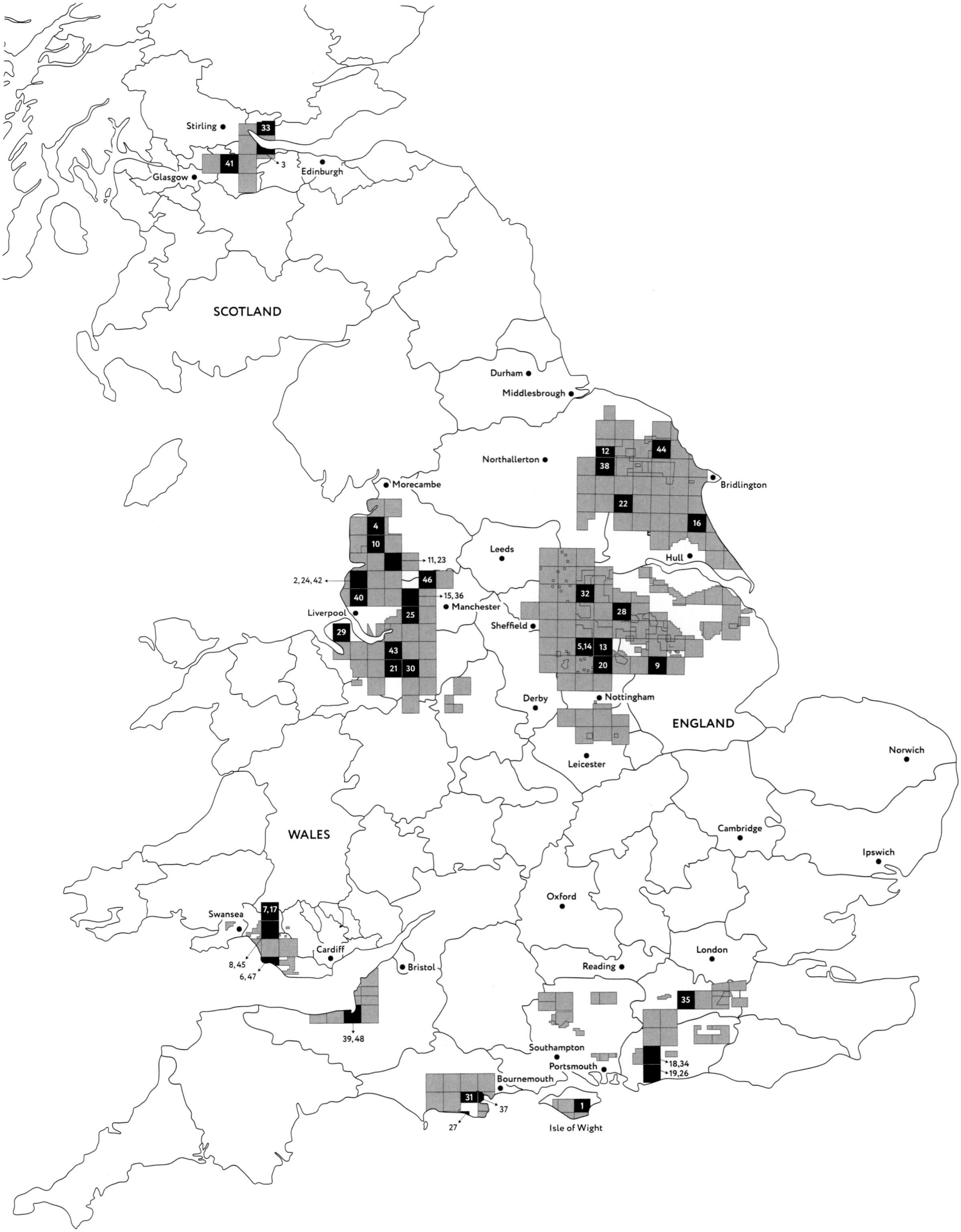

Stirling
33
41
3
Glasgow
Edinburgh
SCOTLAND
Durham
Middlesbrough
12
44
Northallerton
38
Bridlington
Morecambe
22
4
16
10
Leeds
11, 23
Hull
2, 24, 42
46
40
15, 36
32
Liverpool
Manchester
28
25
Sheffield
29
5,14
13
43
21
30
20
9
Derby
Nottingham
ENGLAND
Leicester
Norwich
WALES
Cambridge
Ipswich
Oxford
Swansea
7,17
Cardiff
London
8, 45
Bristol
Reading
6, 47
35
39, 48
Southampton
Portsmouth
18,34
19,26
Bournemouth
31
37
1
27
Isle of Wight

For Barney and Samuel

The images in *Faultlines* portray fragments of contested landscape within the UK Oil and Gas Authority licensed areas under threat from shale gas exploration and extraction using the method of hydraulic fracturing known as 'fracking.' The need to balance the energy security of the nation with the environmental concerns of climate change, industrialization of the countryside, pollution, and biodiversity, renders the debate highly contentious.

The Ordinance Survey (OS) mapping service divides Britain into squares of 100x100km, each having a two-letter reference number, e.g., SD or TA etc. These are further divided into blocks of 10x10km, identified by a two-digit number, e.g., SD51 or TA14. The license areas comprise a varying number of license blocks, with most situated in the North-West and North-East, with some running along the South coastal areas.

Travelling by bicycle and on foot throughout the license areas, the photographs were made between 2015 and 2021 and were inspired by stories gathered from people met. The license block locations of the photographs are marked by black squares on the map

A huge thank you to the following people for their generosity of time and for sharing their concerns:

Carol Anderson, Janice Buckley, Barbara Cookson, John Cosham, Tom Edwards, Debs England, Pamela Foster, Rachel Francis, Lesley Graham, Neil Hickson, Gillian Kavanagh, Ann Kolodziejski, Simon Maxwell, Maureen Mills, Maria Montinaro, Laurence Rankin, Barbara Richardson, Claire Stephenson, Eddie Thornton, Lizzie West, Fiona Williams and Tony Young

A special thanks to Helen Baczkowska for the essay *Not Here, Not Anywhere.*

Thanks also to 'Drill or Drop' and 'Frack-Off Extreme Energy Action Network'.

Thank you to GOST Books for their encouragement, advice and support.

This work was supported using public funding by the National Lottery through Arts Council England.

LOTTERY FUNDED | Supported using public funding by **ARTS COUNCIL ENGLAND**

Faultlines
First published in 2024
by GOST Books, London

info@gostbooks.com
gostbooks.com

Edited and designed by GOST:
Rossella Castello, Katie Clifford, Gemma Gerhard, Justine Hucker, Allon Kaye, Eleanor Macnair, Claudia Paladini, Ana Rocha

Printed in Italy by EBS

British Library cataloguing-in publication data.
A catalogue record of this book is available from the British Library.

ISBN 978-1-915423-31-3